In the
HANDS
~ OF THE ~
POTTER

AN APPRECIATION GIFT FROM
WORLD MISSIONARY EVANGELISM INC.
The Douglas Family

In the
HANDS
OF THE
POTTER

DALE EVANS
ROGERS with Les Stobbe

THOMAS NELSON PUBLISHERS
Nashville • Atlanta • London • Vancouver

Published in Nashville, Tennessee, by Thomas Nelson, Inc., Publishers, and distributed in Canada by Word Communications, Ltd., Richmond, British Columbia, and in the United Kingdom by Word (UK), Ltd., Mil-ton Keynes, England.

Unless otherwise noted, Scripture quotations are from THE NEW KING JAMES VERSION. Copyright © 1979, 1980, 1982, Thomas Nelson, Inc., Publishers.

Scripture quotations noted NIV are taken from the HOLY BIBLE, NEW INTERNATIONAL VERSION ®. Copyright © 1973, 1978, 1984 by In-ternational Bible Society. Used by permission of Zondervan Bible Pub-lishing House. All rights reserved.

The "NIV" and "New International Version" trademarks are registered in the United States Patent and Trademark Office by International Bible Society. Use of either trademark requires the permission of Interna-tional Bible Society.

Scripture quotations noted KJV are from the KING JAMES VERSION.

Library of Congress Cataloging-in-Publication Data

Rogers, Dale Evans.
    In the hands of the Potter / Dale Evans Rogers with Les Stobbe.
       p. cm.
    ISBN 0-7852-8300-5 (cb)
    1. Christian life. 2. Faith. 3. Rogers, Dale Evans. 4. Rogers,
Roy, 1911– . 5. Motion picture actors and actresses—United States—
Biography. I. Stobbe, Leslie H. II. Title.
BV4501.2.R629 1994
248.4—dc20   94-10324
                                                      CIP

Printed in the United States of America
2 3 4 5 6 7 - 99 98 97 96 95 94

CONTENTS

ACKNOWLEDGMENTS   vii

1. ENCOUNTER WITH THE MASTER POTTER   1

2. PLACED ON THE POTTER'S WHEEL   13

3. TRUSTING THE SKILL OF THE POTTER   29

4. THE PAIN OF THE SHAPING   43

5. SLIDING FROM THE WHEEL   63

6. MARRED, BUT NOT BROKEN   79

7. THE RESHAPING OF PRIORITIES   95

8. THE RESHAPING OF PERSONAL AMBITION   111

9. THE RESHAPING OF ABILITIES   129

10. THE RESHAPING OF RELATIONSHIPS   147

11. A VESSEL FIT FOR THE MASTER'S USE   165

12. THROUGH THE REFINER'S FIRE   179

13. ON DISPLAY FOR THE MASTER   193

14. PERFECTED AT LAST   205

ACKNOWLEDGMENTS

I would like to thank my husband, Roy Rogers, our children, and our dear Christian friends, Frances and Leonard Eilers, who bore with us through the early years of our Christian commitment.

My love and deep gratitude to my son, Tom Fox, who by his example led me to a clear commitment of my life to Jesus Christ.

My thanks to Dr. Jack MacArthur, who showed me in a sermon the rightful claim of Jesus on my life.

Thanks also to Reverend Harley Wright Smith, of St. Nicholas Episcopal Church, Encino, California, who told me that Robin would bless our lives and we had made a blessed choice to bring her home from the hospital, and to Reverend O. William Hansen, of Church of the Valley Presbyterian, who has seen us through thick and thin since June 25, 1965, in Apple Valley, California.

Thanks most of all to Jesus Christ, who made my life to shine by sending His Holy Spirit into my heart.

Dale Evans Rogers

1

ENCOUNTER WITH THE MASTER POTTER

*H*ave you ever felt like your world was collapsing, but you were able to put on such a good act that no one could see it? That's what was happening to me in early 1948.

Yes, in 1948, to all my friends the world looked bright indeed for Dale Evans. Only weeks earlier I had added the name Rogers to my name after several years of working with Roy Rogers on the set of western movies. The wedding took place during a blinding snowstorm in Oklahoma on New Year's Eve 1947, and despite the weather the future never seemed brighter. What I didn't know was that the Master Potter was about to begin shaping my life in very painful ways.

Roy Rogers was the brightest star on the western horizon. Already number one in the box office because of his starring roles in dozens of westerns, Roy was in huge demand for personal appearances. Instead of being his leading lady only in westerns, I had achieved what many women dreamed of: I had become his wife. I had also fulfilled another longstanding dream . . . a family. Even as a little girl I had wanted a large family. Although my son Tom from my first marriage had turned into a handsome and successful twenty-year-old, the dream of having a large family had never died. Marrying Roy brought instant family, with his children, Cheryl, Linda, and Dusty (Roy Jr.). (Roy was a widower whose wife, Arlene, died from an embolism following the birth of Dusty.)

The Perfect Life?

Perfect life, right? It should have been, but my world inside was actually collapsing. My emotional burdens were clearly stronger than my inner support.

You see, when I married Roy I lost a major part of my self-identity. The death of his wife had left him with three young children, and I was determined to care for them. In addition, the movie studio decided marriage to Roy meant I could no longer star with him in his movies. Republic Studio had informed me that the children who saw the movies would not believe what they were seeing if Roy and his leading lady were husband and wife in the real world. It would remove the romantic mystique.

I was dumbfounded and struggled with the disintegration of my film career even while I was excited about the new family under my care. From being a movie star, I had suddenly become a nobody, as far as the public was concerned—at least, that's how I perceived it.

That family of three children also provided additional stress. I was having a difficult time being a housewife and a stepmother after having worked for twenty years. Cheryl was seven, Linda was five, and Dusty only sixteen months old when we were married, and they were a handful. Roy worked long hours, leaving me in charge in that most difficult of roles: *stepmother.*

Cheryl and Linda clearly resented my taking their mother's place and, as children will do, made sure I knew it. One day, for example, I was arranging the furniture in the living room when Linda Lou stopped me in my tracks with, "That isn't your furniture. It's my mommy's."

I was alone and on the defensive—edgy and frightened at what else I might experience. I knew I needed more than I had in reserve. What I did not know was that God, the Master Potter, was at work preparing to put me on His Potter's wheel again, but this time I would stick because I was ready to become clay in His wonderful, life-shaping hands.

I had made the decision to accept the Lord as my Savior when I was ten. An itinerant evangelist had come to town and held revival meetings in our church. Again I heard the old, old story of Jesus and His love. This time, however, it was presented in such a dramatic and straightforward way that it really shook my ten-year-old world.

The evangelist opened the gates of hell and gave me a good look at what that future was like. I became so thoroughly frightened at the prospect of spending eternity in such a miserable and terrifying place that I reached out desperately for the hand of the Savior. I reached out in fear, but I was not really ready to hand over control of my life to Him.

I was like a child who cannot swim, but who wants to learn all by herself in the ocean. The child asks her father, an experienced swimmer, to stand on the shore in case the waves overpower her. A cry for help would energize the father so he could jump in and save his child.

I was like that child—I wanted to do my own thing, to become a big success in entertainment. But I also wanted an insurance policy—God the Father standing by, ready to save me if the waves grew too threatening. So when I walked down the aisle of the church and stretched out my hand to Jesus, it was no soul-shaking experience; it was only a matter of laying hold of what I had been told was eternal security. When I was baptized a few weeks later, I felt I had really made it. God would be there when I needed Him, since I had "paid the entrance fees" into His kingdom, the church.

That experience did not, however, stop me from becoming a teenage rebel. I rebelled against my parents' strict Baptist ways, for I knew that they did not approve of my goal of becoming a truly successful entertainer.

Yet, like many teenagers, when I rebelled against my parents, I also rebelled against the Lord. After all, their opposition to my career plans was rooted in the Baptist Church's teaching on what Christians should or should not do with their lives. And singing and dancing on the stage definitely fit the "should not do" category of vocational goals.

My elopement at age fourteen put the exclamation mark on my rebellion. That marriage ended in disaster sixteen months later, when my husband went home to his parents and never returned. When the waves of despair rolled in, I turned to the church and the Bible. As a teenager, I knew I needed more strength than I had to care for our baby son, Tom. I read the Bible through, clinging to it for courage. The Psalms provided a lot of comfort as I grieved over the loss of the young man I still loved, and I sought help for the son now alone in my arms.

Desperation Promises

Several years later when my son Tom appeared to have polio, the waves again threatened to overwhelm me. I turned to God in desperation and promised to live for Him. When Tom's diagnosis turned up negative, I went on with my career, quickly forgetting that promise.

As I struggled for economic survival and up the ladder of success, whenever I was able to have Tom with me I would attend church. After all, I did want him to know the God of my family and experience the love of Jesus. Tom would certainly need that Father on the shore as well. But my attending church did not signify willingness to let the Master Potter shape my life, for I was convinced His plans did not coincide with my plans—and I was determined to carry out my plans.

One of the reasons I was unwilling to even seriously consider letting the Master Potter shape me was a misconception about what God had in mind for me. Shortly after my divorce, I went to business school in Memphis and became acquainted with one of the most beautiful girls I have ever seen. When she became a missionary, I thought, "A missionary? As beautiful as she is, and she is going to Africa? How could she do that?" And I said to myself, "I have to do my thing independently. I am going to make a mark."

Not Now, Lord

I would go to church and hear the preacher say, "If you have talent, it belongs to the Lord." And I would say, "Now, Lord, You don't understand. When I have made it, and when I am independent materially, I will give You my life. But in the meantime I have to work. And, Lord, please look away when I do things that are a little questionable." That kind of attitude had kept me from ever submitting to the Master Potter, but it also contributed to my inner stress.

Tom also contributed to my inner stress. He was still the light of my life, and I was delighted that he had become engaged to a beautiful young Christian woman, Barbara, whom he had dated for several years. But then he announced that instead of pursuing the musical career I had planned for him in symphony work, he had decided to become a teacher of music so he could help children to a career—and to God. For a mother who planned too much and sometimes not wisely, that was a stunning blow. I did not realize that Tom was merely submitting to the shaping of the Master Potter.

Previously when I experienced these crises, I would run to God in my great distress. I would temporarily put myself under His care. But I'm sure the Father must have wondered when I, Dale Evans Rogers, would become willing to genuinely submit myself to the shaping of the Master Potter. If you have had a similar experience, you'll know He doesn't give up easily.

The Turning Point

My turning point came after that encounter with

Linda Lou, when she reprimanded me for moving her "mommy's furniture." Even though I answered her gently, I knew I needed help. So I was ready when Tom walked in and suggested I start taking the children to Sunday school and church—that God could help me do what I was unable to do for myself.

I thought it over carefully. The next Sunday I attended the evening service with Tom. Despite his protests to the contrary, I will always believe he conspired with Dr. Jack MacArthur on the sermon for that evening: "The House That Is Built on the Rock."

The theme did not mean much to me until Dr. MacArthur explained that *any* house built on the rock of faith in Jesus Christ *can* and *will* survive anything that comes up against it—illness, death, poverty, suspicion, greed, selfishness, deceit, lies. I felt like he was throwing rocks at me, and they were hitting me where it hurt. I twisted and dodged and squirmed under the barrage, but there was no escaping it. I sat there looking into my heart and hearing it shout, "Guilty, guilty, *guilty!*"

When Dr. MacArthur finished his message and invited us to accept Christ as Savior, the invitation had my name on it, and I knew it. I knew I should step forward, but I kept fighting the strong urge.

Tom read the story in my eyes. He said gently, "Why don't you go? Why not make it right with the Lord now? Give Him your life, and let Him give you the peace I've watched you struggling for, for so long."

The Battle Was On

I responded defensively, "Tom, I *am* a Christian.

I've been a Christian since I was ten years old. Isn't that enough?"

"No," said Tom bluntly. "You don't really know Christ. I've watched you reading all those 'Peace of Mind' books, and all that Eastern philosophy stuff, and it hasn't helped you one bit. If you really knew Him, all you would need would be your Bible and your faith in Him. You won't find peace until you understand that."

I *wanted* to go down that aisle, but I just didn't have the courage. I knew all too well what was involved, that the Master Potter would then want to shape every area of my life. I had put Him off from age ten till thirty-five, and that pattern of living by my own wisdom was deeply ingrained in me.

On top of that, voices inside were whispering, "All these people will know you're a no-good sinner if you do that. They'll talk about it, and it will be all over Hollywood in twenty-four hours. . . . Don't rush into this thing; think it over for a week or so." I said to Tom, "Give me until next Sunday; I want to think." Tom's eyes filled with tears and pity. He turned away without a word.

Roy was away on a trip, so he couldn't help me. I felt miserable and alone as I drove home. I ran upstairs to my bedroom when I got home, dropped to my knees beside the bed, and cried as I had never cried in all my life. The dam broke, and it all poured out in a long, broken, stammering confession.

When I had cried myself out, I started to pray quietly in a spirit of repentance. My whole past stood up before my eyes, revealing all the lost years like an unrolling carpet. I shuddered at what I saw—sin, sin,

sin—and all because I had refused to know and follow Christ.

I had held God like an ace up my sleeve against the possibility of future punishment. Now I was ready to let Him enter into the tabernacle of my heart, the area that had been locked to Him. I said, "I am opening it all to You. I want You to fill me with Your Spirit, to wash me clean with the blood that You shed for that purpose. Then I want You to use me the rest of my life—whatever it takes."

I cried out in surrender, "God, Lord God, forgive me! Just let me live until next Sunday, and I'll go down that aisle and make a public confession."

He let me live. When the invitation was given the next Sunday morning I bounced out of my pew and fairly flew down the aisle. I grasped Dr. Mac-Arthur's hand and was ushered into a small prayer room for prayer and consultation with a counselor. I repeated my confession, asking God to create a new clean heart and a right spirit in me, to break me if He had to but—please!—to take my life and use it for His glory. I was ready to be on the Master Potter's wheel.

An indescribable peace washed over my heart, washed me clean by virtue of the blood He had shed for me on Calvary, and I became a totally new creature. This time I had made the commitment that Jesus Christ could be the Lord of my life—and that commitment helped me to face all the shaping the Master Potter had planned for me for the rest of my life. My pride had been broken, my intense drive to succeed in life set aside for His plans, and I was ready to heel to the Master.

A New Person

I remember when I came home from church that day—I was flying low. I mean, it was wonderful. The grass was truly greener, the sky bluer, flowers prettier, people kinder. I mean, everything was changed.

Roy noticed it and asked, "What's happened?"

I said, "I have done the most wonderful thing I have ever done in my life. I've given my life to Jesus Christ, to follow Him."

Roy's response revealed he was not yet ready for an encounter with the Master Potter, but God had His eye on Roy as well! When I surrendered to God, He began to fulfill the promise Paul made to the Philippian jailer, "Believe in the Lord Jesus, and you will be saved—you and your household" (Acts 16:31 NIV). I did not know that promise at the time, nor did I realize my action would result in many more than our "household" coming to know Jesus as Savior. God's reward for full commitment to the Master Potter is so much greater than we can even imagine when we take that step.

Yet what does it mean to be placed on the Master Potter's wheel? And why should we be concerned about being shaped by the Master Potter?

Reflecting on the Shaping

1. What has been your biggest objection to letting the Master Potter take over shaping your life?
2. What influenced your decision to turn over your life to the Master Potter for His shaping?
3. How would you describe your encounter with the Master Potter?

4. What was the initial impact on your will and emotions as you let the Master Potter take control?

5. If you feel you have never made Jesus Christ, the Master Potter, Lord of your life, what is keeping you from doing it now?

2

Placed on the Potter's Wheel

*H*ave you ever asked yourself, "Who do I really want to control my life?" Or maybe, "Why should I turn over control of my life to God?"

Strong-willed and determined people like myself know the answer: We must be in charge. We are not going to let anyone else run our lives, unless, of course, we run into a brick wall and discover we are at a potential dead end and need help.

Of course, not everyone is a high-control, goal-directed person. For many the issue of life-control never seems to become a personal crisis. They may be controlled by their parents, who may even determine their vocational goals. Others let friends exercise strong control over them because those friends seem so self-assured and goal-oriented themselves. Then there are those who let circumstances set the pace for their lives. Finally, the Bible says some are controlled by their passions and lusts.

My Hand on My Life's Rudder

You'll remember I set sail on the sea of life with

the rudder firmly in my control, despite having made a decision for Christ at ten years of age. No Master Potter for me. I knew what I wanted and was determined to get it, even after divorce, a son to care for, and a major economic depression that made getting a job extremely difficult. Under no circumstances did I think that God might actually have better plans for me than I did. I saw Him as the spoilsport, not a loving, caring God who recognized my potential and was ready to use my talents.

Does that describe you? Surveys by people like George Barna and George Gallup reveal that there are actually more people than ever determined to be the masters of their fate. That is true even among Christians who, like I did, have attended church regularly for years.

God recognized this tendency in man thousands of years ago and spoke to the prophet Jeremiah about it some 500 years before the birth of Christ.

A Skilled Artisan

First God told Jeremiah to go to a potter's house. Working with clay, the potters made the pages for newspapers and formal records, mugs, lamp bases, pots, and storage containers of that day. They deftly turned lumps of clay into usable objects. Many pieces made in those days can be found in the ruins of ancient cities and help us to discover how the people in those cities lived. We've learned to read ancient languages because clay tablets filled with all kinds of business details and government actions survived fire, floods, and the destruction of war.

So the potter was a key artisan in ancient villages.

He or she shaped what people wrote on; stored food, water, and wine in; and ate and drank from. Of course, not all potters were equally skilled, but all had a measure of control over the lump of clay in their hands.

With that as a backdrop, read what God told Jeremiah: "Arise and go down to the potter's house, and there I will cause you to hear My words" (Jer. 18:2).

So Jeremiah went to the village potter to see what he was making. Unfortunately, having an onlooker must have rattled the potter, for the object he was making did not turn out right. So he reworked the clay and shaped it into another vessel. Jeremiah uses a key phrase to describe that process: "So he made it again into another vessel, as it seemed good to the potter to make" (Jer. 18:4).

That description sets the stage for God's words:

> "*O house of Israel, can I not do with you as this potter?" says the LORD. "Look, as the clay is in the potter's hand, so are you in My hand, O house of Israel!" (Jer. 18:6)*

Who's Really in Charge?

God then asks if it is not within His rights as a potter to relent, to hold back the punishment promised those who sin against Him when they turn from their ways. At the same time, He asserts it is within His rights to bring evil consequences on those involved in sinful actions. Despite the awesomeness of their Maker, Israel chooses to "walk according to our own plans, and we will every one obey the dictates of his evil heart" (Jer. 18:12). Because of that attitude, because of their unwillingness to be the people of God as intended, the land of Israel would be destroyed and made desolate. He was going to scatter them before the enemy like an "east wind."

I did not understand this imagery, this description of His response to rebellion against Him, even though I read the Bible through after my first marriage failed. I did not interpret what happened to me as being in any way the result of my failure to let my life be shaped by the Master Potter.

More than twenty years of aggressively pursuing my own goals for my life had produced a measure of success as the world counts success. After all, I had been the star singer on a national radio program, and I had been the leading lady in numerous western films.

That was not the whole story, however. My broken marriages (see chapter 8) and inability to find personal happiness and joy revealed my bankruptcy of soul and spirit while pursuing my own goals. I had refused to give God control of my life, but I was also beginning to realize that I wasn't as smart or as competent as I thought I was. Maybe the Master Potter had a better idea after all!

Some of you may be saying, "What you're talking about sounds an awful lot like a dictatorship, as though God is some super despot who insists on always having His way. Surely I must have something to say about how I live my life!"

That's exactly how I felt when I was in my teens. I was smart enough to skip three grades, becoming a junior when I was fourteen. I wanted to be a writer, making my best marks in English composition and history. But I also wanted to be a dancer and to be in show business as a singer.

My ego manifested itself very early. When I got hurt, instead of going to the Lord and saying, "I want You to pick up the pieces, please, and put me back together again. Make me what You want me to be," I just straightened my back and said, "I will show You."

How different is the attitude expressed by Isaiah:

> *But now, O LORD,*
> *You are our Father;*
> *We are the clay, and You our potter;*
> *And all we are the work of Your hand. (Isa. 64:8)*

But isn't the idea of God's demanding control over our lives an Old Testament concept? Didn't Jesus bring us a new freedom, a new relationship with God?

Yes, He did. Yet as strange as it may seem, the idea of our being clay and God's being the Master Potter shows up in New Testament writings as well. The apostle Paul made clear reference to it in his letter to the Romans:

> *But indeed, O man, who are you to reply against*
> *God? Will the thing formed say to him who formed*
> *it, "Why have you made me like this?" Does not the*
> *potter have power over the clay, from the same*
> *lump to make one vessel for honor and another for*
> *dishonor? (Rom. 9:20–21)*

A Humbling Experience

Recognizing the right of the Master Potter to shape our lives according to His design is a humbling experience. You have to be humble before God, know that He is God, and know that only He can make your life really count for His glory before you will be willing to accept His shaping. For Christians, it means accepting our weakness, our earthiness, our mistakes, and letting the Master Potter have His way, tough as it may sometimes seem.

I did not recognize single parenting as part of His shaping. Nor did I recognize that God was shaping Tom in a way that would prepare me to yield control to God. As far as I was concerned, my divorces were simply part of the normal tragedies of life—and not part of God's pursuit of me. Like many, I saw these experiences at best as dumb mistakes that I could correct the next time around.

The Benefits Are Real

Here's how the apostle Paul describes what submitting to the Master Potter did for him:

> *We are hard-pressed on every side, yet not crushed;*
> *we are perplexed, but not in despair; persecuted,*
> *but not forsaken; struck down, but not destroyed—*
> *always carrying about in the body the dying of the*
> *Lord Jesus, that the life of Jesus also may be*
> *manifested in our body. (2 Cor. 4:8–10)*

That's the strength, those are the resources that became available to me when I bowed my head and said to the Master Potter, "Whatever it takes, I am committed to Your will in my life for the rest of my life."

"But," you may say, "I'm a little puzzled about when the Master Potter actually gets involved with us. You've said that He really was able to put you on the Potter's wheel only after you bowed in total surrender to His will as a result of Dr. MacArthur's message and your son's prayers. But you also suggested the Master Potter was active in your life while you were still rebellious and determined to go it alone. Are you saying God is involved in shaping us long before we surrender to Him?"

Prepared for Leadership

Yes, I am convinced God is reaching out to us, allowing experiences that will help us develop into the kind of people He can use.

I think of how God prepared Joseph as a boy for his future role as second in command in Egypt during a time of famine. God had Joseph grow up in an agricultural setting, so he understood about abundant crops versus famine. He put him through the extremely negative experience of being sold as a slave so that he could experience God's presence in the worst of times.

God allowed Joseph to be thrown into prison for an alleged sexual advance so he could make the contact that would later lead to his high-ranking appointment. Joseph was on the wheel of the Master Potter all this time, but he really did not know it. Even if he saw some elements of it, he failed to grasp the full implications.

Roy and the Master Potter

God was similarly at work in Roy's life well before he accepted Christ, preparing him for his contributions as an entertainer, especially to children in hospitals and orphanages, and finally as a parent of adopted special children.

No one thought of it as a benefit at the time, but the fact that Roy's mother was crippled played a major role in his life. He developed an empathy for those who are disabled and disadvantaged. As a result, he always had his advance man set up visits to crippled children's hospitals and orphanages when he toured in special appearances. He'd ride his horse Trigger right into the hospital and introduce him to the children. No, Trigger never made a mess on those visits—he was a very well-mannered and trained horse.

Even today, at eighty-two years of age, Roy stays in touch with several disabled children, communicating with them in a variety of ways—despite having sixteen grandchildren and twenty-seven great-grandchildren, with two more on the way.

Roy's home also prepared him musically. Roy says, "I never thought I would be a singing cowboy. I never expected to get into entertainment. Yet at home my three sisters played the mandolin and guitar, as did Mom and Dad when I was little. So I learned to play the guitar. And we'd have square dances and sing and have our own entertainment.

"In 1930 I left Ohio to go to California. The first job I got was picking peaches in Tulare County. When that was over I drove a little Model-T dump truck, hauling sand to a golf course in the Los Angeles area. The guy I was working for lost his trucks, so there went my job. My sister, with whom I was staying, said to me, 'Honey, they have an amateur show on the Englewood radio station every Saturday from midnight to six in the morning. I'll call them up and see if I can get you on it.'

"Being young and straight from the country, it made me sweat just to think about it. But I said okay. So we went up there, and when they announced my name I froze to my seat. My sister came to me and said, 'You get up there.'"

Launched as a Singer

Roy continues, "To this day I cannot remember what songs I sang. But I sang a couple of songs and yodeled. They took my name and address—and I could not get out of there fast enough. I didn't know radio could make you that nervous, because you don't see your audience. Three days later I was called and joined my first group, the Rocky Mountaineers. I was there for over two years, when I organized the Sons of the Pioneers."

Roy also learned to ride bareback on a mule at the age of eight. When he was eleven his father purchased a horse that had been a sulky racer. Again he had to ride bareback. Roy says, "I never rode with a saddle, but, man, I could get on that horse—just grab his mane and swing over onto him. You get the feel of the horse and ride smoother."

I always envied Roy his smooth, natural ride in the saddle, since I had to learn riding as an adult. Roy's experience was just another way God had prepared him for his later role in westerns and at rodeos.

Roy comments, "When I look back on my life, many things have happened that seemed accidental, but as I look back on them now, I know it had to be God.

"One of those things happened when I was with the Sons of the Pioneers on KNX in 1937. I was out at this hat store in Glendale, California, getting my hat cleaned. I was sitting there when a guy just about tore the door off in his hurry to get through it. He started looking around and said, 'Can I get a cowboy hat here?'

"I said, 'I don't know, since I am just getting mine cleaned. What's all the excitement about?' He panted, 'I've got to get a cowboy hat. I have a screen test in the morning at Republic Pictures. They are looking for a singing cowboy.'

"Well, I got my hat and left. I got to thinking about it, and said to myself, 'I just think I'll go there.'

Clearly God's Appointment

"When I got there the next morning, I could not get in. A man told me, 'You have to have an appointment.' I said, 'I don't know anybody, but I've worked here with the Sons of the Pioneers.' But he said, 'You have to have an appointment before I can let you in.'

"I decided to wait. Along came a whole bunch of people back from lunch. Extras. So while he was taking names, I just walked in with the extras. I had just gotten through the door when a hand fell on my shoulder.

"'Hi,' he said. 'What are you doing here?'

"I thought he was going to throw me out. So I said, 'Well, I've just been waiting around. I've been trying to get in all morning. I heard you were looking for another singing cowboy.'

"He said, 'Well, that's why I stopped you. We've been testing these guys. You never once entered my mind. I've seen you over here in Gene Autry's pictures with the Sons of the Pioneers. But until you walked in the door I had not thought of it.'

"I was tied up at Columbia, so I got my release from Columbia, where we were doing backup music with the Sons of the Pioneers. They did the screen test at Republic Pictures, and I was signed up.

"So there are two things that nobody had anything to do with but God."

We don't, of course, establish biblical principles from our experience, but Roy's experience certainly illustrates how intimately God is involved in our preparation for His calling on us.

Chosen Before Birth

The apostle Paul is a New Testament example of how God chooses someone for a special purpose— and then shapes the person very deliberately until he or she recognizes what God wants to do in his or her life. Writing to the Galatians, Paul revealed that God had "set me apart from birth . . . that I might preach him among the Gentiles" (Gal. 1:15–16 NIV).

On what basis did God call the apostle Paul into this special service even before he was born? Paul wrote, "[He] called me by his grace . . . to reveal his Son in me."

So how did God prepare this Jew to be the pioneer in taking the gospel to the non-Jews of his day? Paul was born in Tarsus, a university city in Asia Minor, modern Turkey. Although he came from a strict Jewish family, he clearly was exposed to the Greek world of his day. He certainly studied Greek philosophy, for his sermon at Athens and his letters reveal a thorough acquaintance with it.

As a young man he went to Jerusalem and studied at the feet of a leading Jewish educator, Gamaliel. He described himself in Philippians 3:5–6:

> *Circumcised the eighth day, of the stock of Israel, of the tribe of Benjamin, a Hebrew of the Hebrews; concerning the law, a Pharisee; concerning zeal, persecuting the church; concerning the righteousness which is in the law, blameless.*

Yet this very righteous Pharisee, who was convinced he was doing God's will, needed more than a zeal for God to be available for shaping by the Master Potter. He needed to meet the Master Potter in a very personal encounter. The dramatic story is told in Acts:

> *As he journeyed he came near Damascus, and suddenly a light shone around him from heaven. Then he fell to the ground, and heard a voice saying to him, "Saul, Saul, why are you persecuting Me?" And he said, "Who are You, Lord?" Then the Lord said, "I am Jesus, whom you are persecuting. It is hard for you to kick against the goads." (Acts 9:3–5)*

Now the man who would become Paul, the apostle, was ready for his first shaping experience as a new believer. God sent a very special servant of His, Ananias, whose words resulted in Saul's vision being restored. More than that, Ananias apparently shared with Saul God's revelation that the new convert would be "a chosen vessel of Mine to bear My name

before Gentiles, kings, and the children of Isracl"
(Acts 9:15).

God had thus shaped the fiery former persecutor
of the Christians for a very special ministry. Because
of his Jewish training, Paul was able to go first to the
synagogue as he traveled on behalf of his Savior. He
later reached out to the Gentiles, the non-Jews, in the
community.

A Similar Commitment

A similar commitment prepared Roy for a truly
worldwide influence as a Christian. When I came
home from church after making a public commitment
to Jesus Christ as Master Potter, I had changed so
much that Roy noticed it. He asked, "What's happened?" And I said, "I've given my life to Jesus
Christ. I've decided to follow Him."

Roy said, "I can tell something has happened to
you. But leave me alone. Don't you be working on
me."

There is no doubt that my desire to share my new
joy embarrassed our friends in the movie business. I
wanted everyone to have this peace that I had, the
fantastic release in my spirit that I had experienced.
Everyone, in fact, thought I was a fanatic. I remember
publicity people saying, "You are going to ruin Roy's
career and your own."

We had a party in our home—strictly a Hollywood
party, with a lot of the people in the business present.
I didn't drink, so I did not serve cocktails. I remember
one of Roy's new leading ladies in his pictures notic-
ing my lack of alcohol, and saying, "Evans, whatever

is the matter with you? What has happened to you? You are not the same."

I responded, "Well, I'll tell you. In the first place I have a family with small children. And I made a decision in my life to follow the Lord. I have had an experience with God, and I'm different inside. So I don't enjoy the things I used to enjoy." She just looked open-mouthed at me, since she really did not understand.

Roy had overheard the conversation, and since he had not yet made his decision, he was very angry with me—particularly over my comments about my responsibility for the children. He said, "If you don't like it, this is not the place to talk about it."

I went upstairs and cried. But the next morning he came down and asked me if I was going to church—and he went with us. That night he accepted Christ.

Now I'll let Roy tell his side of the story, how God was at work getting him ready to become clay in the hands of the Master Potter. "Dale did talk to me about what had happened to her. The kids started going to Sunday school. We started saying grace around the table. It would start with the kids, and as it went around the table it got closer and closer to me. I knew that one of these days the kids would ask me. And they did. After several months one of them turned to Dale and asked, 'Why doesn't Daddy ever say grace?'

"I don't remember exactly how it happened, but one day she said, 'Do you want to say grace, Daddy?' So I said my first grace. I had already been to church with Dale. And I was thinking hard about the job she had as a stepmother, and what a terrific job she was doing. One night at church everything the minister said seemed aimed right at me. Everything he said hit me between the eyes—the things I had done and the things I hadn't done. It really woke me up.

"When the minister gave an invitation to come forward and accept Christ, I could not get there quick enough. And I have been that way ever since.

"I think that's the reason Dale and I are still together. We've just had our forty-sixth wedding anniversary because we have the same vision about Christianity, about the way your life feels, and the way you feel about other people. It is just completely different from before."

God used the apostle Paul mightily in proclaiming the good news. In his own way, Roy has consistently maintained a witness for Christ by reaching out to disabled children and spotlighting the hymn or gospel song we sang at every television show or public appearance. With his abilities as a horseback rider and as a singing cowboy, Roy became in the hands of the Master Potter a credible representative for Him.

You may still be skeptical about putting your life in the hands of the Master Potter. So let's consider why we are afraid to trust Him—and what skills He brings to the table that should encourage our trust.

Reflecting on the Shaping

1. How much control have you felt you needed in order to be successful in today's world?

2. Read Romans 9:20–21. Do you believe the Lord has a right to make you into what He wants?

3. Which experiences in your life might be considered the Master Potter's shaping even before you

acknowledged He was the Master Potter, and you the clay?

4. For which experiences are you grateful to the Master Potter right now?

3

TRUSTING THE SKILL
OF THE POTTER

Maybe you've been where I was the night God took drastic steps to get my attention. He had been pursuing me, I realized much later, but I was not about to listen to the Master Potter's call.

I was living in Louisville, Kentucky, and had a position as staff singer at a local radio station. I had Tom with me at the time. Suddenly a polio epidemic hit the area. I came home from the radio station one day to find Tom vomiting and screaming with pain. I immediately took him to the hospital. They ran a long needle down his spine to draw fluid to see if he had polio.

While he was being examined, I paced the corridor, praying, begging God to keep Tom from having polio. I remember pleading with God, "Let my boy be all right! You can have my life, but let me have my boy."

A Miracle

Even though the doctors had been sure it was polio, the report was negative. Based on the symptoms, I can only say it was a miracle that it was not polio. I was relieved, and I went to church, giving thanks to God.

I continued to struggle to survive financially. With the Depression on, I had to take Tom to my folks' farm in Texas, where he would be safe and in school. My mother, who was a remarkable Christian, took over the training.

Like many who make promises during a crisis, I forgot my promise to God, for soon the cares of making a living and providing for Tom again overwhelmed me. God had done His part to get me onto the wheel of the Master Potter, but I quickly removed myself and remained in control.

Relationships are a two-way street. The Bible is filled with examples of God wanting to develop a deep and intimate relationship with people; yet, the people were not ready to let Him into their lives—except in cases of emergency.

In my case, God was there waiting for me to submit to His shaping, to enter into a truly vital relationship with Him. But I thought I could get by with church appearances and Bible reading in times of crisis. What my actions were saying to God was, "I can't trust You with everything I am and want to be. I'm not convinced You are skilled enough and care enough about me as a person to entrust myself to You and Your shaping of me."

Remember the story of the spies Moses sent to check out Canaan? Of the twelve who visited the land God had promised them, ten were in the category of God-doubters. They were convinced that despite the abundant crops and the richness of the land, God could not give them victory over the giants living in the land. Those spies reached that conclusion despite the fact that God had sent the plagues to force Pharaoh to release them from bondage in Egypt. He had divided the water in the Red Sea so they could all march through to escape the pursuing Egyptian army. On top of that, He had let the waters return in time to wipe out the Egyptian strike force. The Israelites had run short of water in the desert only to have God provide water from a rock in response to Moses' command. They had seen God supply manna as a daily provision, and meat as a special provision. Still, they doubted that God could be trusted to help them conquer those living in Canaan.

Only Joshua and Caleb had developed enough trust in God to say: "Let us go up at once and take possession, for we are well able to overcome it" (Num. 13:30).

They were overruled by popular vote. Instead of seeing God provide miraculously for them, all of those original people, except for Joshua and Caleb, died in the desert during the next forty years—only the offspring experienced the bounty God had prepared for them all.

The people of Israel did not change much over the next thousand years. Yes, there were brief periods where they turned to their God, especially during the reigns of kings like David and Hezekiah. But the human tendency to try to run our own show, to worship idols of our own choosing, was demonstrated in them over and over again.

Digging Our Own Cisterns

Isaiah's prophecies about the coming Messiah are

well known, especially since Handel incorporated some of them in his great oratorio *Messiah*. Yet Isaiah also lamented the failure of the people in Judah to follow the Lord, calling them "a rebellious people, / Lying children, / Children who will not hear the law of the LORD" (Isa. 30:9).

That certainly described me. For years I did exactly what Jeremiah accuses the people of Judah of doing:

> *My people have committed two evils:*
> *They have forsaken Me,*
>   *the fountain of living waters,*
> *And hewn themselves cisterns—broken*
>   *cisterns that can hold no water. (Jer. 2:13)*

That's what I did when I eloped with my first sweetheart, even though I was active in church as a youth leader. That spring about six couples from our high school eloped. We went across the state line so no one could stop us. I said I was going to spend the night with a girlfriend but went to my boyfriend's hometown instead. We were married in the home of a Baptist preacher, with his wife as witness.

We took off for Tennessee. I discovered that even though he was four years older than I, my new husband was a thoroughly spoiled boy. His parents were divorced and shared custody. And both had spoiled him. He had never been denied much.

We had a terrible time financially. He had to take a job, after having worked only for his father. After Tom was born, we had to sell my husband's car to pay some bills. He just could not cope. So just before Easter he took me to my mother, who lived in Memphis at the time. His brother and sister said they would come and pick me up in a week. But he never came back. Instead he wrote me a letter saying that he wanted to be free.

I cried for a year. I thought my life was over. I even thought of committing suicide—I was so hurt, so crushed. Since he wanted it, I finally filed for divorce.

While I read the Bible through and gained a lot of courage from the Psalms, I did not really turn my life over to the Master Potter. I was determined to show my ex that I could make it on my own, just as the people of Israel repeatedly left the Lord and dug out their own cisterns.

I took a business course and went to work in Memphis. I started singing and playing the piano at a radio station, developing quite an audience. I was working for Clarence Saunders, the developer of the Piggly Wiggly chain, the first serve-yourself stores. One day I came out at lunchtime, and there was my ex-husband sitting on the curb.

Even though I had cried many tears, I still had a crush on him. So I agreed when he said, "I want to talk with you. See if you can get off this afternoon, and we'll go to the show." I got off, and as we sat in the show he said, "I want you to come back." I said, "My mother will never take me back if you leave me again." He replied, "I'll take out some insurance on my life [so even if something happened to him, I'd be taken care of]. You won't have to worry."

He was so convincing that I agreed to go back with him. But when I went home and told my mother, she said, "If you go back to him, and he leaves you again, don't come home." Since I had my little boy, I had to make a responsible choice—and turned down the opportunity to be reunited.

Later I was thankful to my mother, for my ex-husband became an alcoholic and married two more times, mistreating his wives. One day when his sister refused to go fishing with him, he committed suicide.

Yet even that escape from what surely would have continued to be a terrible marriage did not make me turn my life over to God. Like Israel, I actually became hardened against God, rejecting His overtures of love.

Why Trust the Master Potter?

Why should we trust our Savior, Jesus Christ, as our Master Potter? What evidence do we have that He truly is skilled enough to shape us into whole people who glorify Him?

Let's think of how an earthly potter gets started. He takes clay dug out of the ground, adds water, and stirs the mixture until it has an even consistency. All lumps must be broken down, for they will weaken the object being made. The quality of the clay put on the potter's wheel is totally dependent on the skill of the potter in preparing it for shaping.

What the potter then starts with is a nondescript lump of clay with no particular shape. Only the hands of a skilled potter can shape that lump into a useful object.

Even such a "minor" thing as how the clay is centered on the small platform on the wheel is vital. If the lump of clay is not accurately centered on the potter's wheel, the elliptical action makes shaping a round object impossible. While the resulting object can bring a lot of laughter, it is no laughing matter for the potter.

Knowing how to develop the exact texture in a

lump of clay and how to place it correctly on the wheel so it is easily handled are two critical steps to the successful creation of an object. Only a truly skilled potter can produce a truly beautiful object.

Buyers know which pottery-making friend they can trust to produce a truly well-formed, beautiful object. Their trust has been built by seeing that potter make many beautiful objects. Trust is developed by demonstrated skill.

Let's extend that analogy to human beings in relationship to the Master Potter. Who is this Person who insists on our being the clay while He does His thing as a potter? God described Himself to the people of Israel and Judah through Isaiah, the prophet:

Thus says the LORD, your Redeemer,
And He who formed you from the womb:
I am the LORD, who makes all things,
Who stretches out the heavens all alone,
Who spreads abroad the earth by Myself."
(Isa. 44:24)

Now if during the time I was refusing to let God take control of my life you had asked me if I believed God had created everything, I would have emphatically agreed He was the Creator. That had been drilled into me in Sunday school and in the youth group. But the implications of that did not hit home until many years later.

My musical talents, a gift from God? That's what the preacher kept saying, but He wasn't the one practicing at the piano long hours, learning new songs, adapting my style to that favored by most people.

Trust God with my talents? Not when I had worked so hard to develop them!

And who got me onto radio in Memphis, Louisville, and Dallas? Who got me the opportunity to sing with a group at the Blackstone Hotel in Chicago? Who got me five shows a week as a singer on CBS, with a commercial on Sunday? *I* did, through a lot of effort—and maybe some luck—or so I thought.

Only later did I realize that the God to whom I paid lip service was in reality the Master Designer, the Master Potter. He was at work even during my rebellious years, preparing me for when I would yield control to Him. My twenty-five years of life under my own control have been followed by fifty-nine years under His control—and those have been the truly productive and satisfying ones. But that could not happen until I was willing to truly trust the Master Potter.

He Is Eager to Guide

Yet it is not only the fact that God formed us in the womb for His purposes that should make us willing to trust Him as Master Potter. God did not just create us and then forget about us. In a pronouncement very similar to the one in Isaiah 44, God speaks in Isaiah 48:17:

> *Thus says the LORD, your Redeemer,*
> *The Holy One of Israel:*
> *"I am the LORD your God,*
> *Who teaches you to profit,*
> *Who leads you by the way you should go."*

The Lord adds something I wish I had paid attention to early in my life as an adult: "Oh, that you had heeded My commandments! / Then your peace would have been like a river, / And your righteousness like the waves of the sea" (Isa. 48:18).

That's the Lord who is asking us to let Him be the Master Potter in our lives. That's the Savior who is asking us to trust Him with our future.

One of the men I admire most did that. Leonard Eilers grew up in North Dakota. He had a very difficult childhood. After being a cowboy for some years, he came to Hollywood, where Cecil B. DeMille picked him up to be a cameraman. But God got a hold of Leonard, and he gave up his position to go to the Bible Institute of Los Angeles. After graduation he became a pastor, but his primary ministry was to cowboys in the movie industry.

Leonard Eilers is an amazing person. He never had any big churches. He never had any huge gatherings. He was never a big-time evangelist, and he certainly never became a star. But he was faithful.

Leonard used to liken people to horses. He'd talk about God's having to tame them. He'd do rope tricks while in the saddle for children's meetings, talking about the Lord and "the last roundup." But his most important ministry was to cowboys in the movies, where he was known as the preaching cowboy.

I loved to read what Leonard Eilers wrote, written so beautifully using cowboy language. It just broke my heart that no publisher would accept his writing.

If Leonard Eilers had not been willing to accept the Master Potter as a teacher and attend the Bible Institute of Los Angeles, and if Leonard had not been willing to let the Lord direct his way, I don't know what we would have done when our special child, Robin, was born—and died two years later.

You see, one day soon after I submitted to the Master Potter there was a knock on the door of our big, old Spanish house in Hollywood. When I opened the door, there stood a woman whose husband was a cowboy preacher—and who had been quietly, persistently witnessing to Roy. I hardly knew her, but I invited her in.

Frances Eilers brought a Bible, on the flyleaf of which she had written Proverbs 31. I took her to a famous Hollywood restaurant, the Brown Derby, for lunch. That started an extremely important friendship for me, for God used her to do a lot of reshaping in me. Even more important is the example she and Leonard were to me.

When Robin, our special little angel, died, Frances was the first person I called. She came over and took me in her car and let me cry for two hours while the funeral director came to pick up Robin's body, while Leonard sat with Roy. God really used this woman to bring peace into my life during some of God's most difficult shaping periods.

All of this became possible only because Leonard decided to accept at face value God's promise to teach him what is best, and to direct him in the way he "should go." What a role model he and Frances became to both Roy and me!

A Caring God

The skill of the Master Potter also expresses itself in the attitude with which He shapes us. Tom Peters and his wife frequently remind readers in their book

In Search of Excellence that the difference between a successful, profitable company and one that does not make it is usually a matter of attitude. If everyone is oriented to helping the customer with a friendly, caring attitude, customers will come back again and again.

During the writing of this book, a friend and his wife moved from their own home in California into an apartment in Nashua, New Hampshire, to be close to a son and his family. Any move is traumatic, but one across the country, going from one's own home into an apartment, creates a whole new range of feelings. And since apartment managers can be difficult, they wondered what the response would be when a maintenance problem arose.

To their delight, the complex's sales staff proved to be both friendly and consistently helpful, even volunteering to help move furniture. When my friend's wife turned in a "laundry list" of maintenance problems after taking possession of the apartment on a Saturday, a maintenance representative showed up on Monday to correct all the problems. He even replaced old and noisy equipment—and volunteered to help hang pictures.

My friend thus was not surprised when he and his wife met tenant after tenant who had been in the same apartment for years. In today's world, considerate, caring landlords are a prized jewel.

It took me years to realize that God also is a truly caring, loving Lord. My picture of God had been that of a holy, righteous God ready to whip me in line when I did wrong. Somehow I missed passages like Hosea 11:3–4:

"I taught Ephraim to walk,
Taking them by their arms;
But they did not know that I healed them.
I drew them with gentle cords,
With bands of love,
And I was to them as those who take
*   the yoke from their neck.*
I stooped and fed them."

Only after I submitted to the shaping of the Master Potter did I discover Lamentations 3:22–23: "Through the LORD's mercies we are not consumed, / Because His compassions fail not. / They are new every morning; / Great is Your faithfulness."

That's why I failed to heed His call as I attended churches to make sure that Tom got the right start in life, while refusing to agree to His leading for my life.

Healing the Wounded

God's love, His compassion, and unfailing kindness do not prevent Him from shaping us in ways that at the time are painful indeed. But the pain of the shaping is always matched by the Master Potter's skill in healing the wound.

The fact that God's skill in healing should reassure us is a constant theme in the prophetic writing of the Old Testament. While God comes down hard on disobedience and consistent rebellion, He often reminds Israel that He is the God who heals as well. After Hosea had, on the basis of an order from God, restored an unfaithful, promiscuous wife and accepted her unconditionally, he writes:

Come, and let us return to the LORD;
For He has torn, but He will heal us;
He has stricken, but He will bind us up.
After two days He will revive us;
On the third day He will raise us up,
That we may live in His sight. (Hos. 6:1–2)

Never was that more evident than when I submitted to the Master Potter as a result of Dr. Jack Mac-Arthur's message. The relief I felt, the healing of the soul I received, changed my whole outlook on life. I not only had fellowship with my Lord, but my fears were gone as well. I gained new confidence as a mother of three children, knowing that I now had the Savior and His love with me at all times. I came to understand what the apostle Paul meant when he wrote to the Ephesians:

He would grant you, according to the riches of His
glory, to be strengthened with might through His
Spirit in the inner man, that Christ may dwell in
your hearts through faith; that you, being rooted
and grounded in love, may be able to comprehend
with all the saints what is the width and length and
depth and height—to know the love of Christ which
passes knowledge; that you may be filled with all
the fullness of God. (Eph. 3:16–19)

As the Master Potter began His sometimes painful shaping in my life, I recognized more and more how wide, how long, how high, and how deep is the love of Christ. And I rejoiced in being able to share it with others as I spoke.

The skill of the Master Potter is far beyond my

comprehension, but in time I have learned to appreciate many aspects of it. In the coming chapters I want to share more of what it means to be shaped by the Master Potter, so that you, too, can enjoy the richness of His care and provision.

Reflecting on the Shaping

1. What experience before you encountered the Master Potter personally revealed that the Master Potter could be trusted?

2. Why were Joshua and Caleb so positive that God could be trusted to give the Israelites the victory over the inhabitants of Canaan?

3. Who are some of the caring persons who have helped you recognize the loving care of the Master Potter?

4. What qualities of the Master Potter are important to you after reading Hosea 11:3–4 and Lamentations 3:22–23?

4

THE PAIN OF THE SHAPING

*B*y now you've realized that the Master Potter is deeply involved in each one of us. Before we acknowledge Him and submit to His shaping, He is the "Hound of Heaven," pursuing us in love. Once we submit our lives to Him, the shaping begins in earnest.

When a human potter begins to work with the lump of clay on the wheel, the initial changes are the most radical. After all, the lump is rather shapeless. Only after this radical reshaping can you begin to see what the lump of clay might become.

That initial stage in our lives is described in Psalm 139:15–16:

> *My frame was not hidden from You,*
> *When I was made in secret,*
> *And skillfully wrought in the lowest*
> *   parts of the earth.*
> *Your eyes saw my substance,*
> *   being yet unformed.*

That's what God starts with—an unformed person.

Yet there is no doubt in my mind that when God begins that original fashioning, He most assuredly has an overall plan in mind for our development. Because He has known the end since the beginning, He already knew just how much tempering would be needed to complete the vessel He envisioned. The Master Potter is indeed skillful, and His plan is perfect.

Yet beyond our initial shaping, so we can eventually become the people He wants us to be, the Master Potter often has to engage in major shaping along the way that is quite painful. That seems to be particularly true with those of us who acknowledge Him as Lord only in adulthood. While we were going our own way, running our own lives, we developed in ways that require radical action on His part after we get onto the Master Potter's wheel. Even while on the Master Potter's wheel we may develop a habit that requires special attention on His part—and experience the pain connected with that shaping.

Shaping Is Not All Joy

An example of God's shaping is the apostle Paul, known as Saul until he capitulated to Jesus Christ on the road to Damascus. When Saul set out on that trip to Damascus to ferret out Christians and put them in prison, he was a proud Pharisee. Truly a self-assured, self-righteous person—overweening pride of race and religion motivated every action. God had to employ drastic means to get through to him, as we mentioned in chapter 2. Yet being knocked from his horse and blinded for some days did not make Paul a truly humble person for all time—God knew he had a tendency toward pride. So as part of Paul's shaping, the Master Potter engaged in a little long-term, though painful, shaping.

A Personal Weakness

Isn't it often true that those people who are specially used and unusually blessed and gifted have a personal weakness that the Master Potter has to deal with? The apostle Paul reveals genuine personal transparency about his weakness in his second letter to the Corinthians: "And lest I should be exalted above measure by the abundance of the revelations, a thorn in the flesh was given to me, a messenger of Satan to buffet me, lest I be exalted above measure" (2 Cor. 12:7).

Ouch! That was clearly painful. Certainly this does not seem like a light experience for the great apostle, something he just brushed aside as unimportant, does it? He reports that it was so painful that he asked the Lord three times in great earnest to remove the "thorn in the flesh." Each time God said no, knowing that Paul's special weakness toward personal pride would require lifelong attention. But the Master Potter did give him a promise: "My grace is sufficient for you, for My strength is made perfect in weakness" (2 Cor. 12:9).

I know all about that tendency. I've already confessed that I grew up a proud little girl. Being the first grandchild in my mother's family, my aunts showered me with love, compliments, presents, and advice. I became headstrong, determined to have my own way.

That tendency to pride was not helped when my

mother and aunts taught me to read long before I entered public school. Instead of walking into a first-grade class when I started school, I was put into third grade. That's heady stuff! Later I skipped eighth grade, even though during the seventh grade I had experienced a health breakdown because my schedule was so full. The doctor discovered a spot on my lung, and I had to spend months in bed, totally missing the summer vacation.

I've shared how I eloped at fourteen while still a junior in high school, determined to be the master of my own fate. I wanted to be a singer/actress/dancer, while my parents wanted me to be a schoolteacher or music teacher.

A Matter of Humility

God knew that I had an intense drive to control my own life, so He let me undergo something similar to the apostle Paul's experience on the road to Damascus. The experience of committing my life to the Master Potter as a result of the message by Dr. MacArthur dramatically changed my attitude. But the Master Potter knew that He still had some serious shaping to do if I were to become the truly humble person He wanted me to be—and it would be painful.

My first major shaping after submitting to the hand of the Master Potter began with the birth of our daughter, Robin. I had always wanted to have a large family because my father and mother came from large families. I especially wanted a little girl. Yes, I had a son whom I adored, but I wanted a girl as well. Little did I know what an excruciating experience the fulfillment of that dream would become.

Yet the Lord prepared me even for that experience. We were still living in the old Noah Beery home in Hollywood, with its professional-size tennis court and a badminton court in front. The kids played there a lot.

God's Preparation

One day Linda Lou was playing there with neighborhood children when a tall, blonde woman with a little girl walked by. But this was no ordinary little girl. Little Nancy was on crutches, for she had a horribly disfiguring disease. She had no feet, just huge lumps of flesh, and huge hands. She was wearing what looked like a hoop skirt, only it wasn't—just a long skirt. Yet she had the face of an angel and a truly sweet spirit.

When Linda Lou noticed this mother and daughter watching them play, she called out, "Come in. Come in and see us." She was endowed with unusual gentleness and care for the unfortunate and disabled—not surprising, really, with Roy as her father.

I brought out some cookies and lemonade and invited them into the house. I discovered that the mother had been an art illustrator for magazines, but was now involved in caring for her disfigured daughter.

I could not get over the spirit of Marguerite Hamilton and her daughter, Nancy. There was no timidity despite Nancy's affliction. And they possessed an incredible faith in God, that He would provide for their need. There would be times when they had no bread to eat, but little Nancy would say, "It's all right, Mom. He'll see to it that we have bread when we need it."

Invariably there would be a basket of food left for them. Different churches supported them, but their provision did not always overlap adequately.

Marguerite and Nancy's courage just astounded me. I could not imagine my son, Tom, when he was small, not having money for food, for a doctor bill. I realized later the truth of Jesus' words, "A little child shall lead them."

Pregnant!

We were ecstatic when I became pregnant in 1949, less than two years after Roy and I were married. We prepared like all other expectant parents. I was, of course, hoping it would be a girl. What I did not know was that God was going to give me a lesson in humility. He had to get that veneer of pride off. And the fact that He would humiliate me meant that the Master Potter really cared about me. That did not, however, reduce the pain of the shaping!

The first hint of trouble came in my seventh month of pregnancy. The doctor did a blood count. He informed me that I had an Rh-negative blood factor, while Roy had a positive factor. As a result, our baby might have difficulties because of our incompatible Rh factors.

Robin Elizabeth arrived after midnight on August 26, 1950. Groggy and weak after the birth, I turned my eyes to the glass-enclosed incubator and saw a pretty, delicate little girl kicking her legs. My first question was, "Is she all right?" to which someone answered, "She looks okay." As they wheeled me out, Roy kissed me and said, "Honey, she's beautiful; she has little ears just like yours!"

The next day I complained to the nurse giving me a bath that they were not bringing me my baby as often as they brought other babies to their mothers. And when they did bring her, she was sleeping so soundly that I could hardly wake her up. I also noticed that when I held my baby up to the light, she looked faintly Asian. The nurse avoided my eyes, cleared her throat, and asked, "Are they going to let you take her home?"

I responded indignantly, "Of course I'm taking her home. Is there any reason why I shouldn't?"

The nurse looked at me and said, "Tell your doctor to tell you the truth about her."

My heart began to pound, and I demanded she tell me if there was anything wrong. She could not do that, so I immediately called my doctor and told him to tell me what was wrong with my baby.

Something's Wrong with Robin!

The doctor came and told me that Robin was not responding to certain routine tests. They could not tell how she would progress, but she had been in an oxygen tent since her birth, and that was not good. He suggested we take her home, love her, and enjoy her, because "in cases like this, love does things that nothing else can do."

My heart turned to cold stone. At first I was too numb to cry. I prayed, "Lord, I know You understand this. I don't, but I trust You."

Unbidden, the scene where I had walked the corridor in that Louisville, Kentucky, hospital while Tom was being examined years earlier flooded my mind. I had promised God that if He would save Tom from infantile paralysis, I would put my life in His hands. I flushed with remorse, and promised God that I would not question His wisdom in letting Robin arrive in this condition. Whatever He willed, I would accept.

The pediatrician who was caring for her explained that she appeared to be a mongoloid child (today we call it Down's syndrome). She had the square little hands full of creases, the tiny ears, the undeveloped bridge of the nose, the slanting eyes. When the pediatrician came to the description of the eyes, I told him indignantly that she had Indian blood on her daddy's side, and that would account for the slant in the eyes. I was still in denial and refused to accept his description of Robin.

Most distressingly, we were told to place Robin in an institution as quickly as possible, so we would not become attached to her. She would need special care that we would be unable to give her at home. We refused. We felt that God had sent her to us for a purpose, and we would never find that purpose if we were to put her away. Roy said, "We'll just take her home and love her and raise her as best we can, and trust God for the rest."

The Utmost in Humiliation

Knowing my inner distress, God, the Master Potter, was about to make Himself known to me in a very personal way. He knew what it meant to have a Down's syndrome baby in 1950—especially as a member of the Hollywood community. It was the utmost in humiliation, for people felt there was clearly a weakness in the parents if a child was born with Down's syndrome. Those children were simply kept hidden because society was not willing to accept them. This was true even in churches.

God knew that—and He also knew how He could use me if I would accept the challenge of caring for Robin. But I knew none of that the night we brought Robin home. I was a mixture of feeling sorry for Roy, of worrying whether I was adequate to care for Robin, and deep concern over what Robin herself would have to experience because of her physical disabilities.

Then as I lay in bed I heard Robin singing, as babies often do just before they go to sleep. I thought, "How could anything be wrong with a little angel like that?" But in my heart I knew.

I turned off the bed lamp and lay in the darkness, crying my heart out. Finally I fell asleep, totally exhausted. About two in the morning I awoke with a start. I sensed a definite presence in the room—a presence so pronounced I could almost reach out and touch it. There was no light, just the presence of the Holy Spirit.

As I lay there, enveloped by the presence of God, I was comforted. I knew it was going to be all right, that God was going to be with us through it all. That was definite! I breathed a "Thank You, Lord. I know it is You. I'll be all right now," and went back to sleep.

For a long time I told no one about this experience. I was sure people would not understand. They would think I was out of my mind. But I knew it was real and thanked God for the peace and comfort He had given me.

It is important to realize that this experience with the Lord did not remove the pain of the shaping; it just made it bearable. I still struggled emotionally when I saw how Robin suffered. She was not only a Down's syndrome child, but she also had a congenital heart defect. She would try to pull up in her crib and turn blue and have great difficulty breathing. During her second year, there was a polio epidemic and she caught it, leaving her unable to stand up again.

The Lord's Comfort

The Lord came to comfort me a second time. I had taken Robin up to San Francisco to see a doctor who did research on Down's syndrome children. He was trying to get them to a point where they gained muscle tone. He told me after he examined Robin, "Her heart is almost crowding her liver, it is expanding so fast."

On the way home I was alone with her in the bedroom on the train. I had strapped her in on the upper berth. The major changes in her environment had resulted in diarrhea. She was crying and crying, and I couldn't find any way to stop her. I started crying myself, praying, "Lord, please help me. I cannot stop this child. I am totally helpless."

All of a sudden I saw what looked like a blue haze in the dim light of the room, almost like a curtain. I thought, *Who is smoking on this train?* I opened the drape and looked out—and it was clear as a bell. All of a sudden I felt warm inside, and I knew it was the Holy Spirit. Robin stopped crying and went to sleep, and so did I. I was truly grateful that the Lord honored me with His presence just when I needed Him the most.

The Master Potter revealed His love for me and helped me to bear the pain of the shaping taking place in less dramatic ways as well. Two months after Robin's birth I left for New York to appear on a TV show. I had to change trains in Chicago, so I was browsing in the magazine and book section of the newsstand. I noticed that the current issue of *Reader's Digest* had an article by Pearl Buck called "My Child Stopped Growing." Then I noticed a book by Dr. Norman Vincent Peale, *A Guide to Confident Living*. I purchased both and got back on the train.

The Pearl Buck article rang a bell of hope for my Robin. It described her so perfectly I started to cry. Then I opened Dr. Peale's book to the chapter "How to Meet Sorrow." I devoured it—and it devoured my heartbreak. I promised myself I would someday meet this man of God, who had steadied me and given me courage. He had helped me to realize that God would meet every need as it presented itself. Little did I know how important he would become for the publication of Robin's story in book form.

Time for a Move

When you have a child like Robin, painful experiences seem to come in waves—and never stop coming. For example, doctors told us that Los Angeles and Hollywood were too damp and smoggy for Robin in her weakened condition. We should move to the San Fernando Valley, where the air was more invigorating. So until we found a place there, Robin was to live in the home of her nurse.

One night I came home after taping a radio show to find the nursery bare. I let out a bawl like a cow just deprived of her calf. Roy and the nurse had thought it would be easier for me if Robin were moved when I was not home, but it was instead a big shock. I waited two days before going to see her and was relieved to find her in a lovely sunny room in a home filled with serenity and love. When we found a ranch in the valley, Roy's father and uncle built a little apartment especially for Robin, so she could be cared for adequately.

Despite the Lord's very personal assurances of His love and presence, I still had questions. I asked our pastor, "Why did this happen to us? Is it because of sin, or sins in our pasts? Or is it something I did when I was carrying her?"

Our pastor replied with deep compassion, "These things happen because of cumulative sin over many generations. The Bible says that all have sinned and come short of the glory of God. None of us knows exactly why these things are allowed to happen—only God, and if we trust Him, someday we will understand. This experience will cut away the dross and the tinsel from your life. You will know, once and for all, what is really important in life."

He was right. It was a refining experience—a shaping experience by the Master Potter. I believe it was necessary, even though it was painful, so we could be used more effectively by God. He was certainly teaching me that Dale Evans Rogers was not in control of her life anymore—the Master Potter was. He had purposes for our life that could not have been accomplished if we had stayed the Roy and Dale of the days before Robin Elizabeth was born. Those purposes would start to be fulfilled much sooner than we expected.

An Old Testament Parallel

When I remember our experience with Robin, I

have to think about a young woman in the Old Testament, Hannah, who also wanted a child badly. What wouldn't she have given for a large family!

The Bible reveals that hers was a very religious family. Every year Elkanah would take his whole family to the tabernacle at Shiloh to worship Jehovah. He would give Peninnah, one of his wives, and her children portions of the meat after the sacrifice. But because of his special love for Hannah, he would give her, who appeared to be unable to have children, a double portion.

That act of love apparently only increased Hannah's unhappiness that she could not bear Elkanah any children. On top of that, Peninnah was jealous of her husband's love for Hannah and did whatever she could to irritate Hannah. As the years went by, the irritations increased, and Hannah's unhappiness caused her to have the equivalent of an emotional breakdown. The Bible says she wept constantly and could not eat.

The pain of her shaping by the Master Potter was so great that even her husband's many manifestations of his special love for her did not satisfy Hannah. Only a child would do. So she made a vow to the Lord in Shiloh:

> "O LORD of hosts, if You will indeed look on the
> affliction of your maidservant and remember me,
> and not forget Your maidservant, but will give
> Your maidservant a male child, then I will give him
> to the LORD all the days of his life, and no razor
> shall come upon his head." (1 Sam. 1:11)

It had taken years, but the Master Potter had

achieved His purpose with Hannah. No longer did she need to have a child to shut up the jeering Peninnah. No longer did she need to have a child to feel she was a proper wife to Elkanah. Now she wanted a child so she could give him up to the Lord's service. The fact that no razor was to touch his head meant he would be totally dedicated to the Lord (a later example is John the Baptist).

When Eli heard Hannah praying, he thought he was dealing with a drunken woman. But Hannah assured him she was indeed sober, for "out of the abundance of my complaint and grief I have spoken until now" (1 Sam. 1:16). Eli responded kindly, "Go in peace, and the God of Israel grant your petition which you have asked of Him" (1 Sam. 1:17).

Shaping a Son for Service

God did answer Hannah's desperate prayer and gave her a son. She named him Samuel, delivering him to Eli for tabernacle service when he was old enough. Yet in a truly unusual way, Hannah must have also been used by God to help shape the young child for God's service. He was still only a young boy when he heard the voice of God and was used by God to bring Eli the bad news about judgment on his family. Based on what we know about Eli's wicked sons and the indulgent priest, it is difficult to think that Samuel had become responsive to God because of the influence of Eli and his sons.

Yet even that shaping for God's service must not have been without a lot of pain; to be separated as soon as they were must have grieved Samuel as much as it did Hannah, despite their commitment to serving God.

In time, Samuel became God's messenger to Israel's first two kings. He first was sent to King Saul repeatedly to share both God's wishes and God's judgment with the king. Then God used Samuel to discover and anoint King David for his service as Israel's king. We do not know whether Hannah was still alive when these events took place, but if she was, I'm sure she must have praised God for how He was using her son.

During this extremely difficult time with Robin, I, too, rejoiced over how God was using my son, Tom, and his wife, Barbara. During his music studies at the University of Southern California, he became a highly skilled instrumental musician. Upon their marriage, he and Barbara moved to Yreka, California, where he took a teaching position and directed the music in a church. Six months after Robin's birth, we rejoiced with Tom and Barbara over the arrival of their first baby, my first natural grandchild, Melinda Christine Fox.

Yet even in this the Master Potter was at work shaping both Tom and Barbara and us. Tom and Barbara soon noticed that one of Melinda's legs seemed shorter than the other, that it seemed to drag when she tried to crawl. After examination, a pediatrician revealed she was missing one hip socket. I had a stab of pain in my heart every time I watched that little girl and her leg.

Tom and Barbara seemed to have more faith than I did at that moment. They were convinced that God would handle it. Through Roy's contacts with the

Shriners, they were able to take her to the San Francisco Hospital for Crippled Children.

I went with them, praying desperately that God would perform a miracle. With pounding heart I watched them attach a steel brace to her shoes and slide her leg into it. This was to force the leg into the hip to form its own socket. God answered prayer, and today Melinda walks as easily and normally as the rest of us. In retrospect I can see it was just another way in which God helped shape my trust in Him, though again the shaping brought pain before the praise!

More Involvement—More Pain

When Claudia, Robin's dedicated nurse, left us because of exhaustion, we hired a fine Christian nurse named Ruth. Just at that time Robin became restless, refusing her food, and taking only milk. She cried almost constantly.

One day her face swelled and her temperature soared. She had caught the mumps, even though we had kept her segregated from the other children who had the mumps. A pediatrician came and gave her a shot, but she steadily got worse.

The doctor who had examined her after her birth came to our house and he leveled with me. He said that the infection had gone to her brain. She had encephalitis, and he doubted that she would make it. Even if she did, there would be severe brain damage.

I asked him, "If a miracle should happen and she should make it, would it be possible to do open heart surgery on her and close up that congenital defect—

the hole in her heart? I will spend my last penny to help her."

He smiled sadly, shook his head, and said, "No, she would never survive the anesthesia. Keep her as comfortable as you can, and go on loving her, and learn from the experience. That is what I would do, if she were my child."

Although said kindly, the doctor's words were like the signing of a death warrant.

Near midnight I was awakened by spine-chilling howling and wailing. I threw on a robe and rushed to the family room to find Lana, our German Weimaraner dog and Robin's special pet, trying to get outside. I remembered the stories of dogs wailing as death approached someone they loved, but Roy did his best to deliver me from that idea—it was just a myth.

Robin's fever was frighteningly high, and her crying was almost more than I could bear. In the morning Ruth dipped her in and out of cool water. We took turns walking her and bathing her face, but she slipped into a coma. The doctor came, shook his head, and said there was nothing we could do.

At four in the afternoon I remembered that the children had not had lunch. I went into the kitchen to fix something for them. They were very quiet. While I was standing by the sink, the Lord again let me know He cared about my pain. I distinctly heard Him say to my heart, "I am going to take Robin." I said, "All right, Lord. As You will."

I went back to Robin. She was breathing with an ominous rasping, rattling sound in her throat. I was dimly conscious of a bird singing in the eaves of her little house. It seemed to me that Robin and I were suspended between two worlds. Lana, the dog, scratched wildly at the screen door in a last desperate effort to get inside. She yelped the same bark she used whenever she stood between Robin and a stranger. The nurse sent her away. I stumbled blindly out of the door for a breath of fresh air, and to pray. Roy and I walked a bit. With tears streaming down my cheeks, I asked God to take her quickly and not let her suffer anymore. The nurse soon came out and said quietly, "She's gone."

Robin had gone to be with the Master Potter. She had lived just two days short of her second birthday; we had to put away the wrapped birthday gifts. Friends came, and a flood of phone calls and telegrams began.

With the funeral, a new phase in the Master Potter's shaping began—a phase that catapulted me to international leadership in the movement to help retarded (special) children. And the book the Lord gave me, *Angel Unaware*, opened the doors for that ministry.

Shaping by the Master Potter. Sometimes radical. Usually accompanied by pain. Yet the outcome can be a new humility, a willingness to depend on the Master Potter, to live by His plan for us, and a new ministry for Him.

On the other hand, there may also be a less positive reaction. We can actually be reacting negatively to His shaping and begin sliding from the wheel. But more about that in the next chapter.

Reflecting on the Shaping

1. When you agreed to the Master Potter's shaping, what area of your life did He appear to tackle first?

2. Which experience, though painful, proved most decisive in dealing with this area of your life?

3. How did the Master Potter deal with a key weakness in the apostle Paul's life, according to 2 Corinthians 12:7?

4. If you had a major traumatic experience that dramatically reshaped a key area of your life, how did the Master Potter prepare you for it?

5. Describe one answer the Master Potter gave you to your questions during that major reshaping.

5

SLIDING FROM THE WHEEL

*H*ave you ever felt you had lost touch with God? That you needed to send out an all-points missing-person bulletin to see if God could be found? What was happening to you just did not mesh with your concept of a loving God, so obviously He wasn't around and wasn't involved.

I felt like that when our adopted Korean daughter, Debbie, was killed in a bus accident on a church-sponsored trip near San Clemente, California. She had just turned twelve. I had committed my whole life to Jesus Christ, putting myself into the hands of the Master Potter, fourteen years earlier. We had walked with the Lord during the pain after Robin's birth as a Down's syndrome child, and her death two years later. He had personally reassured me with His presence at two critical times in Robin's short life. And God had used her book, *Angel Unaware*, to release a floodgate of opportunities to witness for Him.

Debbie had been a gift from God to our family. Now she was gone, in one of those senseless accidents that provide no answers for grief-stricken parents.

It's not as though I needed more trauma either. Roy was in the hospital for a spinal fusion. There he had developed a staph infection, and he had been in real danger. My whole being was focused on getting him well and back on his feet. Then came the news of the bus crash.

Roy could not help me with any of the arrangements. They had just moved him to the convalescent hospital the day Debbie was killed, indicating he was out of real danger. But very quickly a problem developed and they had to take him back into the acute care hospital. So I was left without Roy's help in making all of the funeral arrangements and the family arrangements.

God held me up during the hectic days of getting ready for the funeral, during the funeral, and the things I had to do right after the funeral. Yet two weeks later I began to slip.

Emotionally Vulnerable

Roy was still in the hospital. I was looking through Debbie's clothes alone, her little toys and other things. All of a sudden the devil really tempted me.

"Do you think God really cares about you?" he asked. And in that unguarded moment I let his whisper become a shout in my thoughts, just like Eve in the Garden of Eden. I began to slip off the Master Potter's wheel, to doubt that there was any purpose in this senseless death of a loving, promising daughter.

I was working on the closet in which Debbie's clothes were hanging. I closed the door and squalled for about three hours. I could not stem the tears as I complained to God, "I don't like what You have done.

I don't think it is fair, and I do not see any reason for it. I just don't get it."

I was fast slipping from the Master Potter's wheel when I went into the kitchen to cook supper. I began to work in the kitchen, banging pots, pounding on the stove, letting my anger run full course—I was really airing my grievances to God.

My mother, who had come for Debbie's funeral, came into the kitchen. She grabbed me by the shoulders and said, "Frances [my given name], sit down here. I am ashamed of you. Where is your faith?"

I turned to her and asked, "Mamma, did you ever lose a child?"

"No," she said.

"Then you don't know," I said. "You don't understand. You just don't understand what I am going through."

Then she said, "Sit down. Let me talk to you."

I sat down.

"Do you know how Debbie loved flowers? She was always picking me flowers from other people's yards on her way home from school. God's garden is the world, and people are His flowers. He has a very big house, so He wants flowers for His house.

"Sometimes He picks one that's mature, with the leaves already falling. Sometimes He picks one that has just opened. And sometimes He picks one that is only a little bud. God has simply picked your Debbie while she is a little bud. He is the Gardener. It's His home, so doesn't He have the right?"

Back in His Hands

Through my mom's words, the Master Potter gently put me back in the center of His wheel and continued His shaping process. I had begun to slip because I had started to question His loving purpose for Debbie—but also for Roy and me and the other children. Restoration came when I stopped complaining and recommitted myself to His shaping for my life.

The psalmist Asaph similarly began to slip off the Master Potter's wheel. Asaph describes what went on in his head in Psalm 73:2–3, 5:

> *But as for me, my feet had almost stumbled;*
> *My steps had nearly slipped.*
> *For I was envious of the boastful,*
> *When I saw the prosperity of the wicked. . . .*
> *They are not in trouble as other men,*
> *Nor are they plagued like other men.*

Slipping . . . slipping . . . slipping . . . almost gone. A person at that point says, along with Asaph:

> *Surely I have cleansed my heart in vain,*
> *And washed my hands in innocence.*
> *For all day long I have been plagued,*
> *And chastened every morning. (Ps. 73:13–14)*

Is this kind of questioning of God's purposes in a time of great trauma simply the result of spiritual immaturity, of deliberate turning against God? Not necessarily; we may be slipping off the Master Potter's wheel because of more than spiritual reasons.

When Satan Attacks

Consider the young mother whose divorce has just

become final after her husband walked out on her—an all-too-common experience today. I can certainly relate to that, since my son, Tom, was only an infant when my high school sweetheart husband abandoned me. Like most mothers single because of divorce, I cried buckets for a year. I still loved him, wanted him back, even though I was angry that he had tossed Tom and me aside like something useless.

You'll remember that I had given my heart to Jesus at age ten. I had been very active in the youth group at our church, becoming a leader as a very young high-schooler. I knew that the Bible had the answers. So I determined I would read the Bible through in a year—and I did. Yet, amazingly, I cannot remember gaining much from it except comfort from the Psalms, since they contained many expressions of outrage that matched my own.

That Bible reading had no significant impact on how I behaved over the next twenty-five years. It did not change my priorities in life—I remained determined to make a name for myself as an entertainer. It did not establish guidelines for my choosing another husband, for I never used biblical principles in selecting a mate in subsequent marriages (see chapter 8).

Why did Bible reading have so little impact on my life? Was it because I was so young when I began? Not really, for I was already a junior in high school and loved literature and history. Was it because I had so little biblical background against which to assimilate biblical information? Not really, for I had been so active in Sunday school and youth work that I had a basic biblical framework in place.

A significant reason, but not the only one, was my emotional upheaval as a result of my first husband's leaving—and my having to file for divorce myself. That emotional trauma is also the reason for the inability of many newly divorced single mothers to assimilate the heavy doses of spiritual wisdom we keep trying to share with them.

A Matter of Energy Levels

You see, God made us truly unique as human beings. He built into us specific levels of energy for physical activity, intellectual activity, emotional activity, and spiritual activity. When we are, for example, involved in heavy physical activity, we talk about being "drained" and too tired to do anything until we regain some energy. We don't like to talk, read, or even pray.

Similarly, when we experience severe emotional trauma—for me, events like my husband's leaving me with a baby, the death of Debbie while Roy was in the hospital—for you, perhaps the loss of a house in a flood, hurricane, or tornado, even a teenage son's or daughter's arrest and conviction for drug use or burglary—we become "drained" of energy as well.

During that time our physical energy may be almost zero—we've used up so much emotional energy it's a huge effort just to get out of bed. Our intellectual energy may be extremely low; we don't even want to think about what we'll make for supper, much less read a book. Similarly, our spiritual energy may be so low we cannot even pray. We may read the Bible, but remember nothing—and the truths that normally leap off the pages of the Bible don't mean anything to us.

No wonder Satan approaches us at such times of extreme emotional distress. We can't think straight, so his simple, direct suggestions seem to make sense. Repeated, they begin to wear a groove in our brains, enjoying a life of their own. This would never happen if we were not experiencing emotional trauma.

When my mother sat me down to help me get perspective on Debbie's death, she did not give me an involved spiritual argument. Instead, she painted a picture of a little girl bringing home flowers, a most familiar scene, and of God picking a flower for His garden. With my limited intellectual capacity at that moment, since my energy had been used up in my emotional upheaval, I could see and understand the implications of that picture. It made sense to me and restored my faith in a loving God.

Notice how the psalmist Asaph describes his emotional upheaval from distress over the success of the unrighteous and the struggles of the righteous.

Thus my heart was grieved,
And I was vexed in my mind.
I was so foolish and ignorant;
I was like a beast before You. (Ps. 73:21–22)

That certainly sounds like someone whose emotions were using so much of his intellectual energy that he could not think clearly. Until, of course, he entered the place of worship, the sanctuary of God. That calmed his heart and his spirit, letting him begin to think clearly. That's when he saw what God really meant to him:

Nevertheless I am continually with You;
You hold me by my right hand.

You will guide me with Your counsel,
And afterward receive me to glory. (Ps. 73:23–24)

He recognized that the Master Potter's plan is truly the best, that nothing that happens is outside the love of God. With basic assumptions like that, he could let the Master Potter put him back in the center of the wheel.

Oh yes, what about the wicked? Suddenly that was not as important to Asaph as what God meant to him, for he took two verses to describe the fate of the wicked and four verses to express what God meant to him. Instead of Asaph's being on slippery ground, sliding off the Master Potter's wheel, he says:

Surely You set them in slippery places;
You cast them down to destruction.
Oh, how they are brought to desolation,
    as in a moment! (Ps. 73:18–19)

Once you have your head on straight about God, your emotional healing also accelerates. So the last verse of the psalm reveals Asaph's renewed commitment to the Master Potter:

But it is good for me to draw near to God;
I have put my trust in the Lord GOD,
That I may declare all Your works. (Ps. 73:28)

We're Still Not Perfect

Another factor that entered into my slipping from the wheel of the Master Potter is one we are all subject to: our sinful nature. I'm an old-fashioned Christian, and I believe in original sin. I believe it is inside us. We have a spiritual nature as a result of the new birth, but we retain our human nature.

During times of crisis, or when we succumb to temptation, the human nature takes over and we rebel against God. We consciously slip from the wheel of the Master Potter. Then, because we don't want to repent of our sin, we stay off the wheel—until the Holy Spirit chastens us enough to move us to repentance.

When I cried out against God after Debbie's death I rebelled for a few hours only. I never doubted that God was there, but I was hurt and could not understand it. I was trying to fit what He was letting happen into my understanding. But there is no understanding God.

If we release what is bothering us to Him, He may give us understanding in other ways—usually much later, after He has been able to shape us more into His image. Once we have responded to His tap on the shoulder, He will not be satisfied until He gets us back. He certainly has done that for me.

What restored the psalmist Asaph's faith in a just God? Did his priest engage him in a lengthy theological dissertation? There's no record of that. He entered the sanctuary of God, we read in Psalm 73:17. There he was clearly overwhelmed by the sovereignty and justice of God. In quietness before God, his focus changed from jealousy over the success of sinners to recognition that he did not have to worry about God's system of justice. What really counted was where you ended up in eternity, not how much you thought you got away with during earth's short lifetime.

More Reasons for Sliding

Yet, you ask, what about those people having achieved a certain celebrity status in the world, who seem to go on the wheel of the Master Potter, only to slip off rather quickly?

I believe the answer is found in Jesus' parable of the sower. He describes four kinds of people who hear the Word of God and, from the public's point of view, have made a decision for Christ. The first kind hear the Word, but the devil, Jesus says, comes and takes away the Word from their heart. That's because the seed of the Word fell along the hard path, Jesus reveals, and the birds come and eat it up.

From my perspective, this describes people who grew up in a Christian home, attended church regularly, heard the Bible message proclaimed, and made a public decision for Jesus Christ because it seemed the thing to do. Their hearts were never really softened to the Savior; in fact, they may actually have been hardened through what they saw other Christians do, or by what they experienced in the church. So their profession of faith is a cultural act, possibly to get approval. They never were on the wheel of the Master Potter—they only appeared to be. So when Satan and his cohorts (the birds of the air) tempt them sexually or with alcohol or drugs, with money and power, they listen and succumb.

Satan teaches these folks how to rationalize their behavior as "normal," so they may stay in the church community and give the impression that they are Christians and on the wheel of the Master Potter. Amazingly, some even begin to preach the gospel because of the recognition it brings, hoping no one will discover their secret (and sometimes not so secret) sin. Unless they truly repent, they cannot genuinely believe and be saved.

According to Jesus, the second category of hearers is those who "when they hear, receive the word with joy; and these have no root." They believe for a short while, but then fall away.

In the parable, this seed falls on rock, shoots out roots, but soon withers and dies. This kind of hearer may actually agree to be on the wheel of the Master Potter, but slides off during a time of testing.

I've seen this kind of hearer of the Word among celebrities. At an evangelistic campaign, through the witness of a friend in the movie or television community or a member of a professional sports team, these folk make a public commitment to Jesus Christ. Unfortunately, before the Word can take root in their hearts, before they are aware of the subtle dangers of public ministry, they are invited to share their testimony at all kinds of public events. At times they are paraded as prize specimens of God's power to save, even though they have very shallow spiritual roots.

Unfortunately, as anyone involved in such public ministry knows, such persons will experience many disappointments within the Christian community. These new Christians quickly discover that there is glitz without substance even in the Christian community. There are users and abusers—and hangers-on, along only for the glamour or the money.

They have not yet matured enough as believers to realize that Christ is the only perfect one, the one after whom they should model their lives and behavior. Their disappointment at what they experience in the Christian community sickens them and may cause them to turn their backs on Christ. They quickly slide off the wheel and all too often disappear from view as Christians.

The third type of hearer of the Word described by Jesus is the person who apparently starts out all right but is soon stumbled by the thorns of "cares, riches, and pleasures of life." Such a person never bears mature fruit. Only too quickly these people get caught up in a relentless round of activities that leave them less and less time to develop their relationship with the Master Potter.

They develop their own priorities, their own agendas, independent of God's will for their lives. Family worries, business worries, instant success, and addiction to pleasure crowd out their quiet times, then prayer, then fellowship with believers.

These folks are just too busy to give time to God. They are too busy for just being in His presence and listening. There is much talking, but very little listening. Yet you can hear His still, small voice only when you are quiet.

You'll hear these people say, "I made a decision for Jesus Christ," but they have no real fruit to show for it. I fit this category until I made my commitment to turn my whole life over to the Master Potter!

I rejoice for those in whom the seed of the Word has fallen on good soil, who hear the Word, accept it as true and valid for them and their lifestyles, and become fruitful in their witness for the Master Potter. I believe this became my category when I finally let the Master Potter put me on His wheel at age thirty-five.

I find it fascinating to see how God responds when we slide from the wheel of the Master Potter. I know He is genuinely disappointed at our rejection of His shaping. But instead of tossing us on the pile of waste, He lovingly and painstakingly pursues us. This process is best described in "The Hound of Heaven," a narrative poem by Francis Thompson.

I was miserable the first time I read it. It was an absolute picture of me running from God, the "Hound of Heaven," but I did not realize that until later. Only later did I recognize God's patient pursuit of me until I was willing to make Jesus Christ Lord of my life, and I saw ways in which He pursued me. God had developed an insider, a "mole" in spying terms, in the person of my son, Tom. My concern had been that he get the same kind of religious training I had received, but I had no idea God would use that concern, clearly planted by the Master Potter Himself, to win me for Himself.

You see, whenever I was able to afford to have my son, Tom, with me, I went to church with him. I believed this would be good for him. Sure I had to listen to many sermons presenting God's claim on my life, but I had developed hardened ears for that message. I could tune out any personal message because I wanted to stay on my agenda.

When he was ten years old, Tom gave his heart to Christ. He was very gifted musically, so as a young man he studied instrumental music at the University of Southern California. While still a student, he became associate director of music at Jack MacArthur's church. Ever since he had accepted Christ, he had been praying for me. He got people at the church to pray for me. He kept inviting me until I was ready to attend his church—and that's where the "Hound of Heaven" caught up with me.

God uses other tactics as well to get us back on the

wheel when we have taken ourselves off. He may use guilt, for it is the Holy Spirit's job to convict us of sin. We may miss the fellowship with others, for there is nothing in the world like the fellowship of true followers of Jesus. And we certainly don't have the warm assurance of God's presence that we experienced when we were on the Master Potter's wheel. Finally, we won't have the rest that only Jesus can give.

Resting in His Hands

Even today there are times when I get too busy for God. I lose the peace I had, and I ask myself, "What is wrong here? Why did I turn to my own devices instead of asking for God's help?" Naturally the Lord quickly restores His peace when I pray and invite Him to resume His shaping of me.

I love the promises of God for those who stay on the Master Potter's wheel. The writer of the book of Hebrews reminds us: "Therefore do not cast away your confidence, which has great reward. For you have need of endurance, so that after you have done the will of God, you may receive the promise" (Heb. 10:35–36).

I am looking forward to receiving what the Master Potter has promised, for He is truly faithful in fulfilling His plan for us. The admonition to persevere applies to another facet of being on the wheel of the Master Potter. For any number of reasons, a potter may have to set aside an object that is developing nicely because it has been marred. In the next chapter, we'll examine why a vessel may be marred—and how the Master Potter can reshape it.

Reflecting on the Shaping

1. Describe a difficult experience during which you felt you were slipping out of the loving hands of the Master Potter.

2. What insight does Psalm 73 provide regarding the times when we begin to slip from the Master Potter's wheel?

3. Examine Jesus' example of the soils into which the seed of the Word of God falls (Luke 8:4–18). Which kind of soil have you been?

4. As someone may have been of special help to you when you felt you were slipping from the wheel of the Master Potter, who might benefit from your insights and experience?

6

MARRED, BUT NOT BROKEN

*I*f you have ever baked a cake or cookies, you know that not every cake and not every cookie will be perfect. If you are making them for a special occasion, you will select only the perfect cookies and set the rest aside, let your children eat them, or even throw them out. If only one turns out imperfect, you might eat it immediately.

When you bake a cake, it might turn out too brown. No problem—you can cover it with pretty icing, and no one will know the difference. If it is too dry, you serve it with a sauce. As a cook, you know how to rescue even the imperfect cake, for you have invested too much energy and too many ingredients to destroy it.

Now imagine yourself as a potter. You're working diligently to mold the original lump of clay into a beautiful, symmetrical shape. You are putting the finishing touches on it when a loud noise causes you to jump just when your fingers are working on the inside of the top of the vase. Your reflex action causes your hand to pull back sharply—and leave a deep gouge in the soft clay on the top of the vase. The symmetry of the vase has been marred, and it will take a special effort to correct the gouge and restore the vase to its original shape. Yet you are determined to do so, for in your mind's eye you can still see how it ought to look.

Some of us have less patience than others. The less patient person quickly gives up in disgust, setting aside the marred vase or decorative ornament so he or she can start on a fresh project. Rather than putting in the time and effort needed to restore the marred area, they reject the object they have been working on.

Just like the potter working on the vase, the Master Potter is at work shaping us to fit His purpose for us. Yet events in life can cause us to make moves that may for a time force Him to treat us like a marred vessel. He may actually need to suspend His shaping process while He works to restore what has been marred.

A Temporary Relapse

Deep disappointment in what God lets happen may cause a temporary reaction that can cause such marring. Roy, for example, was very close to Debbie, and she just adored him. So when she was killed in a bus accident, he had great difficulty accepting her death.

One Saturday night some weeks after her death we stayed overnight in Roy's parents' house in Van Nuys, California. We planned to go home to Apple Valley very early so we could go to church the next morning. Just before we left, Roy was sitting at the kitchen table. Suddenly he said, "I don't like it. I don't appreciate it. I see no earthly use that Debbie was taken. If that's Christianity, I don't want any part of it."

I said, "God have mercy on you. You don't mean it."

Roy said, "Yes, I do."

He truly believed God had no business letting Debbie die. After all the effort World Vision had made to get her to us and the loving care she had received in our home, she was gone. She was an unfinished vessel as far as Roy was concerned. At that point, Roy pushed away the loving hand of God, and he was a marred vessel for a time.

Now notice how God set about restoring the marred vessel. The next morning Roy and I returned to Apple Valley, and we went to church. Pastor Bill Hansen, then our preacher in the Presbyterian church we attended in Apple Valley said in his sermon, "Don't be afraid of tomorrow, of taking turns, or turning corners in your life, because when you turn that corner, God is there." On his way out of church, Roy shook hands with Bill and said, "You must have been reading my mail. You were talking to me this morning."

As we left I said to Roy, "Do you remember what you said last night?"

"Yes," he said, "God knew I did not mean it."

God knows our hearts, even though our humanness gets in the way. So He sends messengers who help us get our eyes back on the Master Potter.

Possible Permanent Marring

Potentially more devastating can be an incident in which we are personally responsible for injury to another person. My mother told me a story about Dr. George Truett, the great Southern Baptist preacher, that illustrates this. Dr. Truett and a friend were on a hunting expedition. His gun went off accidentally, and he shot his friend, who died later that day. That could have marred him forever, for the sense of guilt that this kind of accident creates can cause us to react so negatively that God has to set us aside.

Yet Dr. Truett was able to accept what had happened as something that God, in His divine sovereignty, had let happen. As a result, God was able to shape him into an even more effective vessel than before. His preaching became significantly more powerful.

My feeling is that people who have been restored, who have experienced God's marvelous forgiveness, have a fresh anointing. They have a new sense of the forgiveness and grace of God. Out of gratitude and love for the Lord, they are more powerful than ever.

King David is a classic example of that in his affair with Bathsheba. Now you really have to think back on how long God had been shaping David before that event.

You'll remember that David was a shepherd boy, the youngest of eight brothers. He seemed to have developed an unusually powerful relationship with God while tending his father's sheep. Not only can we imagine him writing a song or two that later became part of the Psalms, but we also know he tackled the wild animals that were determined to make off with his sheep. He told King Saul:

> *"Your servant used to keep his father's sheep, and when a lion or a bear came and took a lamb out of*

*the flock, I went out after it and struck it, and
delivered the lamb from its mouth; and when it
arose against me, I caught it by its beard, and
struck and killed it. Your servant has killed both
lion and bear; and this uncircumcised Philistine
will be like one of them, seeing he has defied the
armies of the living God." (1 Sam. 17:34–36)*

Amazingly, his brothers didn't seem to be aware of their "little" brother's heroics. When they first heard him speaking to some of the soldiers about Goliath and questioning what the reward was for killing him, they were outraged. Doesn't the following sound like an echo of how Joseph's brothers felt about him?

*"Why did you come down here? And with whom
have you left those few sheep in the wilderness? I
know your pride and the insolence of your heart, for
you have come down to see the battle." (1 Sam.
17:28)*

God's Shaping for Crisis

David did not turn tail and run; the shaping God had given him in the hills with the sheep had turned him into a fearless warrior. We all know what he did to Goliath with the strength and skills God had let him develop while he was being shaped as a shepherd.

David's shaping continued during his time as a fugitive from King Saul. Again and again he and his men escaped the pursuing army of the king. An incident that shows off his character development is the time when he and his men hid deep in the recesses of a cave, only to have King Saul and his officers choose the same cave to rest in. David's guards came back to tell him that King Saul and his men were now deep in their sleep near the mouth of the cave. David's men told him: "This is the day of which the LORD said to you, 'Behold, I will deliver your enemy into your hand, that you may do to him as it seems good to you'" (1 Sam. 24:4).

David crept toward the sleeping King Saul and cut off a corner of his robe. His men were obviously incensed that he had not taken the opportunity to plunge a sword into his enemy and kill him. But David insisted that he could not do that to "the Lord's anointed."

This is the man who became king of Israel after Saul was killed in battle. He led his troops in an assault on Jerusalem and made it his capital city. He was then about forty years old, and, like the kings of his day, he accumulated wives and concubines as part of his retinue. So he had ample opportunity to indulge his sexual desires within the framework of the law of the day.

Temptations of Success

God had blessed David richly, and he knew it. He had become a national hero, and he clearly basked in admiration. Success like that has built-in temptations that only those in the closest fellowship with God can handle. Although David had been shaped by God through truly difficult experiences for his role as king, he, like many who attain positions of leadership, had become a marred vessel.

The pride generated by success is a powerful

weapon of Satan. Power, even in Christian leadership positions, can dull us to the clear commands of God. In David's case he was at home enjoying the perks of power while his men were at war against the Philistines.

Walking about the roof of his palace one evening, David saw a beautiful woman bathing. He was extraordinarily excited by what he saw—and he clearly did not run from temptation. Instead, he inquired who she was. He discovered that she was the wife of a soldier in his army, a soldier currently engaging the Philistines in battle. Desire overcame discretion, and he invited her to his bedroom and slept with her, the disloyal wife of a loyal soldier. In that act of adultery, David became a marred vessel.

The campaign against the Philistines kept Uriah, the husband of Bathsheba, at the front for weeks and weeks. Then Bathsheba discovered she was pregnant and sent a messenger to let David know of their problem. Like most who see the potential of exposure, David devised an elaborate cover-up. He called Uriah home from the battlefront, knowing that the average soldier would be extremely anxious to have sexual relations with his wife. Uriah came home, but refused to sleep with his wife; for he did not want privileges his fellow soldiers encamped in tents in the open field did not have.

Thwarted, King David devised Plan Two. He sent Commander Joab a letter, asking that Uriah be sent into the heat of the battle where he would be killed. Loyal soldier Joab carried out his king's request, and Uriah was killed. David waited until a decent mourning period had passed, and then took Bathsheba as his wife.

God's Program for Restoration

How does God deal with a marred vessel? It's really tough for those of us raised on today's standards in the church to accept what God did to restore David. We routinely cast such vessels aside, convinced they have been irrevocably damaged. Only rarely will we make the effort to restore such a marred vessel.

The Master Potter, however, was not through with his marred vessel. He sent the prophet/teacher Nathan to King David. Jesus later recommended the same first step in Matthew 18:15 for Christians who have fallen into sin. Notice also how and what Nathan communicated to his king, again like Jesus' style of communication centuries later.

Instead of quoting chapter and verse from Exodus 20, and then hammering home the gravity of David's sin with other biblical passages, Nathan told a story:

> *"There were two men in one city, one rich and the other poor. The rich man had exceedingly many flocks and herds. But the poor man had nothing, except one little ewe lamb which he had bought and nourished; and it grew up together with him and with his children. It ate of his own food and drank from his own cup and lay in his bosom; and it was like a daughter to him.*
> *"And a traveler came to the rich man, who refused to take from his own flock and from his own herd to prepare one for the wayfaring man who had come to him; but he took the poor man's lamb and prepared it for the man who had come to him."*
> *(2 Sam. 12:1–4)*

The result? Notice the immediate response of the king after hearing the story: "So David's anger was greatly aroused against the man, and he said to Nathan, 'As the LORD lives, the man who has done this shall surely die! And he shall restore fourfold for the lamb, because he did this thing and because he had no pity'" (2 Sam. 12:5–6).

Now Nathan makes his point: "You are the man!" In effect, Nathan is saying, "David, you are a marred vessel. God's corrective action involves serious consequences for your whole family. Everyone will suffer as a result of your sin. And one day your offspring will duplicate your sin—except they will do it with your wives."

Not a Private Sin

David learned that sexual sin is not private sin. It always draws in the whole family, with dreadful long-term consequences. But God does not toss the marred vessel aside. He begins the process of restoration immediately when David says, "I have sinned against the LORD." Nathan responds, "The LORD has also put away your sin; you shall not die." The immediate consequence, of course, was that David also lost the child conceived in adultery, a consequence all too common even today.

Was David's repentance genuine? Here's what David prays in Psalm 51:10–11:

Create in me a clean heart, O God,
And renew a steadfast spirit within me.
Do not cast me away from Your presence,
And do not take Your Holy Spirit from me.

Why a Story?

Great story, isn't it? But why did the prophet Nathan tell a story when faced with such obvious sin, with such a marred vessel? Because stories help us to see ourselves without destroying our dignity as individuals. Once we see ourselves we make our own application. This type of correction leads to repentance, instead of the anger and further rebellion that characterize much of our correction of sinners when we present them with the facts of God's law. Stories have healing qualities that hard-nosed facts about ourselves do not.

Marred vessels litter the Christian landscape today. Christian leaders God used powerfully for many years, whom He used as vessels to bring honor to Himself, have succumbed to the seduction of sexual temptation. Some of them were national leaders, with powerful media ministries. They discovered that even though the Master Potter had been effectively shaping them for many years, they were not on guard against a sneak attack by the enemy.

Panic, Peter, and Renewed Peace

The classic New Testament example of being marred but not broken is the apostle Peter. It is instructive to again consider how the Lord had been shaping this impetuous fisherman/businessman. Peter was so committed to Jesus, he so clearly understood what Jesus was all about, that he became one of the three in Jesus' inner circle.

Peter had seen Jesus heal his sick mother-in-law. He was with Him when Jesus raised the daughter of

Roy and Dale on set of Susannah Pasa.

Roy and Dale's wedding at Flying L Ranch near Davis, Oklahoma, New Year's Eve, 1947.

Dale with her mother, Betty Sue Smith, and her father, Walter Smith, Dale's son Tom and his fiancée, Barbara Miller, 1947.

Dale in hospital after birth of Robin Elizabeth, only child born to Dale and Roy, their "angel unaware."

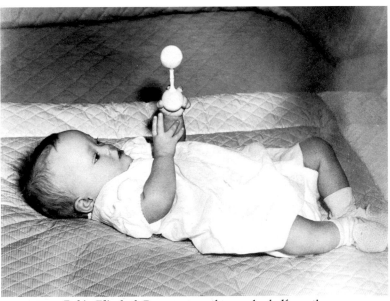

Robin Elizabeth Rogers, at age four-and-a-half months.

Roy, Trigger, Pal, and Dale.

Dale and Gabby Hayes on set of motion picture at Republic Studios.

Dale with Jimmy Durante and Gary Moore on Jimmy's television show.

Don Ameche, Dale, Charlie McCarthy, and Edgar Bergen on "The Chase and Sanborn Hour."

Dale "towing" Pal, a gift palomino from Roy.

Dale on Buttermilk, a buckskin quarter horse ridden by Dale in Roy and Dale's television show.

The Rogers family: (bottom) Dusty and Sandy, (middle) Roy, Debbie, Dale, Dodie, (top) Linda, Marian, and Cheryl.

Dale on "Praise the Lord" with Paul and Jan Crouch, Tustin, California.

Jairus from the dead. When Elijah and Moses appeared on the Mount of Transfiguration with Jesus, Peter was one of the three who experienced it. He saw demons being expelled from people, five thousand or more fed with two loaves and three fish, the Lord's calming the storm on the sea. In fact, Peter had walked on the water in response to Jesus' invitation.

Peter was a hard-core convert—no waffling. He was so committed that he drew his sword and tried to kill a member of the Temple guard, cutting off his ear. He did not care who knew that he was a follower of Jesus.

Until, that is, Jesus was arrested and taken into the court of the high priest. Then all his bravado disappeared, and a scared Peter slipped into the courtyard of the high priest. He sat down with the small crowd around the blazing fire. When the leaping flames lit up Peter's face, a servant girl thought he looked familiar. She looked more closely and then said, "Hey, guys, this man was with Jesus." But Peter denied the association. What you do on the Mount of Transfiguration and what you do when identification with Jesus could mean imprisonment are two different things. If you've ever told a lie because someone backed you in a corner, you know what happened with Peter. He panicked and blurted out, "Woman, I don't know him." She backed off, and Peter nervously wiped his brow. Whew, that had been close!

Just when Peter thought he was home free another person recognized him and said accusingly, "You also are one of them."

What would you have done? Bolted? Hoped they would not catch you as you ran into the darkness outside of the courtyard? Peter decided the best defense was to go on the offensive: "Man, I am not!" he exploded. Again the person backed off.

Time dragged by. Would they ever release Jesus? Why was it taking so long? An hour went by, when a third person told those around Peter, "Certainly this fellow was with him, for he is a Galilean."

If I had been Peter, I would have been gone this time. I mean, three times and you're out! I guess Peter figured bluffing had worked twice, so maybe it would work a third time.

"Man, I don't know what you are talking about!" he almost shouted.

A Wake-up Call

The cock's crowing accomplished what the three accusers had been unable to do—Peter got out as fast as he could. Peter remembered that Jesus had predicted that he would deny Him three times before the cock crowed.

But where do you go now that you've turned coat and denied three times that you had any association with Jesus? Well, first you repent; the Bible says that Peter wept bitterly. Then he rejoined the other disciples, knowing only too well that he was a marred vessel. It appears he kept his experience to himself, but the Master Potter knew.

When Jesus arose from the dead, the angel at the tomb told the women to go tell the disciples—and Peter. And when Jesus joined the disciples at the Sea of Galilee, Peter's net was just as full as that of the other fishermen. And it was Peter whom Jesus engaged in that wonderful interaction about "Do you love me?" Jesus clearly affirmed that Peter was back on the Master Potter's wheel when He said, "Feed my sheep."

Maybe you have not been able to identify with either David's sin or Peter's denial of his Lord. But you've experienced another kind of marring, the kind that happens when you make a commitment to Jesus and then run scared and beat a hasty retreat. You suddenly realize you cannot lead the junior high Sunday school class—they are making hash of your efforts. Or you signed up for short-term service with a mission organization, only to panic when the insects and snakes appeared or when relationships with others in the group quickly deteriorated. You're a failure— marred for life.

John Mark, probably a close relative of Barnabas, had accompanied Paul and Barnabas on their first missionary journey. *What a privilege*, I suspect he thought, as he saw God do miracles on the island of Cyprus. To be with these two giants of the faith must have been exciting. In fact, it apparently got too exciting, for we discover that John Mark turned tail and ran while they were in Pamphylia.

Impossibly marred, said Paul, when Barnabas wanted to take the young man with them on their second missionary expedition. *Not so*, said Barnabas. *He should be given a second chance.*

No way! emphasized Paul, pounding the table. *He lost his chance*. John Mark was branded a quitter.

Another Marred Vessel Restored

Barnabas and Paul agreed to disagree, and each went his separate way. Except that Barnabas took John Mark along to let God restore what had been marred—the courage of the young man. Barnabas the encourager clearly proved successful, for we read in Paul's Second Letter to Timothy, written toward the end of Paul's life: "Only Luke is with me. Get Mark and bring him with you, for he is useful to me for ministry" (2 Tim. 4:11).

The marred vessel had been restored. He was again fit for the Master Potter's use.

Marred, but not broken—if that's how you have been feeling, thank God that He can restore you. He can make the marred vessel beautiful and useful again because of His abundant mercy and grace. All we have to do is repent, seek His forgiveness, and move forward in the power of the Holy Spirit.

We've considered sliding from the wheel, as well as being marred while on the wheel of the Master Potter. What happens when we stay on and let the Master Potter do His shaping? We'll discuss that in the next chapter.

Reflecting on the Shaping

1. If you have had an experience that resulted in a break in your relationship with the Master Potter, what triggered it?

2. Based on the account of King David, tell how God responds when a person who is truly devoted to Him succumbs to temptation, then confesses.

3. What is it about David's repentance in Psalm 51 that made him again acceptable as a leader of Israel?

4. What are the steps a seriously marred Christian

needs to take to be restored, for the marred vessel to be reshaped into something beautiful again, based on the examples of King David and the apostle Peter?

7

THE RESHAPING OF
PRIORITIES

*H*ow is the Master Potter at work reshaping priorities? Does He do it only as we read the Bible and pray? Does He use friends, and even our enemies? Or does the Master Potter sometimes just burst into our lives and dramatically reshape what we're about?

It seems there are several levels at which priorities are reshaped. The most dramatic reshaping of priorities often occurs at the time we commit our lives to the Master Potter. There may also be a reshaping of vocational priorities at one or more stages of our lives. And when we wander away from the priorities once they are established, He attempts to stop us and begin reshaping them once again. At least, that's how I've experienced it—but is there biblical basis for it?

Possibly the most dramatic biblical example of God's reshaping a person's priorities is found in the book of Acts. In an earlier chapter we presented the apostle Paul's illustrious background as a pure Pharisee, with his zeal for Jehovah demonstrated in the intensity with which he persecuted people of the Way. As far as Paul was concerned, the purity of the Hebrew faith and the ethnic expression of it were in danger of eroding if this new sect gained a strong foothold. Having people of the Way, or Christians, as they were first called at Antioch, killed was the only way to prevent the infection from spreading.

Saul's first priority, as he saw it, was to create such terror, such fear of being arrested among people of the Way that they would back off and become a silent minority. With arrest warrants in hand, and accompanied by a party of similar Jewish zealots, he headed north to Damascus.

New Priority Announced

The Lord looked down at this party of zealots and set about changing priorities in a dramatic way. A blinding light flashed from heaven. Saul fell to the ground and heard a voice questioning his priorities: "Saul, Saul, why are you persecuting Me?" (Acts 9:4).

That produced a counterquestion related to authority: "Who are You, Lord?" (Acts 9:5).

The answer must have totally confused this Hebrew zealot, for it questioned all of his assumptions about Jesus. Once considered a figment of people's imagination, the symbol of a false cult that threatened society, the name *Jesus* now represented a new kind of authority.

"I am Jesus, whom you are persecuting. It is hard for you to kick against the goads" (Acts 9:5).

Then came the kicker. "Arise and go into the city, and you will be told what you must do" (Acts 9:6).

No ifs, ands, or buts were permitted. Get up and go. You will get new marching orders. That new priority was presented first to Ananias, who presented it to Saul: "Go, for he is a chosen vessel of Mine to bear My name before Gentiles, kings, and the children of Israel. For I will show him how many things he must suffer for My name's sake" (Acts 9:15–16).

After Saul's conversion, his priorities changed from following his own ideas to listening for the leading of the Holy Spirit. No longer was he Saul of Tarsus, an imposing figure of human intellect and prideful arrogance, but Paul, a lowly servant, willing to move in keeping with the Master Potter's commands. He had embarked on the path of humility, so that eventually he would say:

> *But what things were gain to me, these I have counted loss for Christ. Yet indeed I also count all things loss for the excellence of the knowledge of Christ Jesus my Lord, for whom I have suffered the loss of all things, and count them as rubbish, that I may gain Christ. (Phil. 3:7–8)*

So it happened with Saul, who became Paul, the apostle to the Gentiles. But does it happen today as well? Does the Master Potter initiate that kind of major reshaping of priorities even today?

Yes, especially if you have a totally wrong set of priorities from God's perspective. The Lord's "voice" for me was Dr. Jack MacArthur, my Ananias was my son, Tom. Just as Saul seemed to have known enough about Jesus to recognize what the Master Potter was all about, so also I knew enough about what God wanted of me. I just had to accept that His will was best for me, that His priorities were more important than mine.

God had to get me to the place where I recognized

that God is the only one who can make my life count. He let me experience failure in the area that counted most to me—my family—as I experienced failure after failure in marriage. Yet He let me have success in my career long enough to let me know that it never would satisfy me. Only He could satisfy me. My way simply was not good enough. No one's way is good enough, for only God's way is perfect. Because of that I was absolutely miserable, as though a civil war were going on inside. What I did not realize was that, just as a lot of Jerusalem believers must have been praying for Saul's conversion, a growing number of Christians were praying for me.

My son, Tom, began praying very specifically for me when he was sixteen. He asked a friend who attended a Bible study at the ranch owned by Leonard and Frances Eilers to pray for me. The Eilers had others praying for me as well. I'm convinced that's why I was so miserable.

Possibly because I knew what had happened to Saul, that he had become a missionary to the Gentiles, I labored under the delusion that if I heeded God's call I, too, would have to become a missionary. I would probably, I thought, need to go to innermost Africa. As far as I was concerned, that would be a waste of my talents. Little did I know that God's plan for me would take me as a "missionary" to Americans and the British instead, and that the talents and abilities He had given me fit into that plan perfectly.

What Was Important Changed

When I came back to the Lord, the things that had been so vital to me were no longer important. It's not that I thought, "Now I will be humble." Rather, I had a different center. As Jesus clearly teaches, he that is forgiven much, loves much (see Luke 7:41–47).

Very early in my Christian experience, God showed me where my focus should be when I used the talents He had given me. We had helped found the Hollywood Christian Group. Dick Halverson, for many years the Chaplain to the U.S. Senate, was the first executive director. He understood Hollywood people, for he used to sing with dance bands before coming to know Christ.

At one of our meetings, Dick sang a hymn in a popular singing style—quite different from how it was normally sung in church. I was blown away. A new Christian, I walked up to him and said, "Dick, I didn't know you could sing like that." He looked me right in the eye and simply said, "Praise the Lord."

I thought, "What is the matter with this man? Is he nuts? Can't he take a compliment?" But I understand him now. Praise is hard to accept. It is harder to accept than criticism, because it can get to you. Criticism stings and makes you look to see if it is right.

Dick's response to my comment changed the way I responded after a concert. I never gave a concert after that without pointing my finger up at the finish. What I was saying was, "Never mind me. I'll give the praise to Him."

Change in Family Priorities

When I said to the Lord, "I'm Yours, shape me as You will. Whatever it takes, I'm willing," I also did not realize He would change my family priorities. Yes, I did recognize that His first priority was the family He had given me in Roy's children. They were very important to me. They remained my first priority even though I was eventually invited back to do several more westerns as Roy's leading lady (due to public demand). But I wanted more children of my own.

God said, "Okay, I'll give you a little girl. But I'll use her to change your priorities on family." When Robin Elizabeth was born with Down's syndrome and a congenital heart defect, He awakened more than the usual mother instinct in me. Coupled with my experience with Nancy Hamilton, the little girl with the enlarged feet and hands, he opened my eyes to the needs of what we then called "retarded" children; today we call them special children, or children with disabilities.

I had wanted a little girl to be proud of and to show off—every mother does. After all, I had to keep up my image of success. God knew that would just feed my pride, so He sent me a little girl society was not proud of and kept hidden. When publicity people would come to our ranch to take pictures, they left Robin out of the pictures at our request. I was brokenhearted that I could not show off my special little girl like other mothers did. But God used that to teach me humility, that He had special love for those who need us the most.

When we had Robin, Roy and I faced a critical decision. I was thirty-five and he thirty-six when we married. I was Rh-negative, and he was Rh-positive. Even though the doctor said that our next child could be fine, we decided not to take the chance. We decided to adopt children, especially since Roy's first child, Cheryl, had been adopted and was doing well.

God truly works in amazing ways as the Master

Potter. He started shaping my desires even before Robin died. About four months before Robin died, I had to go to Texas because of the illness of my father. While there, my sister-in-law accompanied me to Hope Cottage in Dallas, where Roy had found Cheryl, and I wanted to find out more about where she had come from.

Preview of Coming Attractions

While at Hope Cottage, we asked if we could see the babies. Looking them over, my sister-in-law said, "Frances, come here and let me show you something. Now, if I was going to adopt a baby, this is the baby I would want."

There lay a baby with light olive skin, big, vigorous and piercing eyes, and blue-black straight hair. She was everything Robin wasn't. Robin was like a little blonde angel. So I looked at this baby and said, "She's cute, isn't she?" I noticed her eyes following us all over the room.

That was in April, and Robin died in August. Soon after Robin died, Roy and I had an engagement in Madison Square Garden. We had to go—we were under contract. We stopped off in Texas to visit my mother just to get away from things. So Roy said, "Why don't we go to Hope Cottage and see the babies?" I said, "I don't want to think about another child. I want Robin." I was in the throes of "I don't want to talk about another baby." Eventually I said, "Okay, if you want me to go, I'll go."

When we got to the cottage steps, I said, "I wonder if they still have that little Indian baby." They had told me that she was Choctaw Indian, and Roy is part

Choctaw. I rushed in to the nurse and asked her, "Is she still here?" The nurse said, "Yes, she is, Mrs. Rogers. She has just finished all her tests, and she's a winner. She's the pet of this place."

I left Roy and ran to where the babies were. I saw her and picked her up, and she jumped around in my arms. Roy came in, and I turned to him, "This is our child." He said, "Are you sure?" I said, "I'm sure." He responded, "If you're sure, I'm sure."

When we talked to the matron, we discovered that the baby had been promised to a woman of influence in Dallas who had Indian blood. She was also coming to see the baby. I said impulsively, "She doesn't need her. We need her. She's never had a child, so she does not know what it is like to lose a child. We need a child. And she needs us. We have a family she will fit into." The matron said, "We'll see."

Success!

When we got to Madison Square Garden we received a phone call from the matron: "Mary is yours. We decided to let you have her."

We let out a war whoop—you could have heard us on Madison Avenue. I was so thrilled. Mary became Dodie when she joined us.

Remember, this was 1952, before all kinds of rules were established that make it almost impossible for families to adopt children. So you'll understand what happened on our way home from New York.

We had stopped in Cincinnati to do another show. There was a note at the motel to call such and such a phone number. For some reason Roy called the number, and the director of an orphanage answered. Roy asked, "You wouldn't have a boy four or five years old, or two or three, would you?" Roy was concerned that Dusty had no brothers—he had all those girls coming at him.

"Well," the director said, "we do have this little boy, but he has a number of things wrong with him, and I don't know if you would be interested."

Sandy had been terribly neglected and abused as a baby. He'd had rickets and had been abandoned three times before he was eight months old. Both parents were alcoholics and felons, and their three children had been placed in different homes.

Roy said, "Can you bring him to the show tonight? I'll have a guy waiting for you."

The director answered, "I'll be glad to." This woman had a daughter paralyzed from her waist down, and she had started the home because of her. Her little girl had watched us on television and wanted to see us. So her mother agreed to bring the little boy.

Howdy, Pardner

Roy came off the show that night, and there stood this little boy with the smile of an angel beside the little girl. The little boy stuck out his hand and said, "Howdy, pardner." Roy was overwhelmed.

We talked about that little boy for three hours that night. He had spent eight months with braces on his legs because of the rickets. The director said he was all right mentally, but a little slow in his reflexes. His walking and running were still not quite free or normal. So we wondered if we could really help him become a normal little boy. Would it be fair to the other children to bring another "special child" into our home after the experience with Robin, and with Cheryl about to enter adolescence, Linda Lou about eight or nine, and Dusty six?

Roy said in a dreamy voice, "Anybody can take a kid that's healthy, but who will take him? We'll take him if we can get him."

The next morning at nine we stood before a judge, signed the papers, and walked out of the courtroom with a brand-new son.

We drove out of Cincinnati with him. Then we picked up Dodie in Dallas and flew into Los Angeles with two new children in our arms. Talk about having the Master Potter change your family priorities!

We've got pictures of the expression on Dusty's face when we came down the airplane steps with this little boy whom we had named Sandy. He seems to be saying, "I don't know if I am going to like him. Does he want to take my place?"

Becoming Brothers

That summer Roy took them both on a fishing and hunting trip. For two weeks they roughed it. They washed their clothes on the banks of the river, went swimming, and slept in the same sleeping bag. When they came home after two weeks, they were brothers. If someone said something bad about one, he got a whipping from both of them.

Life was not all roses with Sandy. He had a hard time trying to ride a tricycle. He was afraid to climb any high place. He had periodic spells of dizziness and vomiting. He also had enuresis, involuntary bed-wetting, which was extremely trying for all of us. He was quite unable to awaken to go to the bathroom during the night, and we had to put on fresh bed linens every day. Many times I wept in shame over losing my temper with Sandy, especially when I remembered his unfailing good humor and sweet disposition. Yet Dusty and he had great fun together. Dusty made allowances for him, for he had been conditioned by Robin to understand handicaps.

Dodie was prone to croup. Remembering Robin, I watched Dodie like an old mother hen watches her one chick. There was a history of tuberculosis in her background, and I did not want to get that started.

When do you stop growing as a family? God had changed our priorities by having us add a native American girl and a physically disabled boy to our family. Going to Great Britain to help Billy Graham with his campaign brought us in contact with another future member of our family.

In Edinburgh we met Chief Constable William Merilees, who was the queen's personal guard in Scotland. He had read my book, *Angel Unaware,* and came to see us. He thanked us for writing the book, since his first grandson was a Down's syndrome child. He said in his broad Scots brogue, "I want you to see my children." He was active in the Church of Scotland orphanage called Dunforth and told us, "I want to take you out there to see my kiddies, and then we'll have an ice cream." So on Sunday afternoon we went to the home.

Our Family Goes International

There we met Marion, thirteen at the time. Her parents were divorced when she was a little girl. The children had been split up, and she had been put in this home. At fifteen she would be able to decide which parent to stay with. Marion had a husky voice and sang for us in a thick Scottish burr, "Who will buy my pretty flowers?"

I was overcome and started bawling and crying. It was Dodie's first birthday, and I was not home to be with her. Roy was moved as well. So we asked if we could take Marion to the U.S. for just a goodwill tour, as a child who had impressed us the most as an orphan. She came over the following summer.

Once in America, she asked if she could stay and go to school for a semester. So we got permission to keep her until Christmas. Then she wanted to stay until June. Finally we received permission to be her foster parents until she was twenty-one.

Then we heard about Korean orphans, so we contacted Bob Pierce of World Vision. We were filling an engagement at the Houston Fat Stock Show when a letter came from Bob Pierce, with a picture of a little Korean orphan he thought might fit into our multicultural home. She was named In Ai Lee, and had a Dutch bob, soft brown eyes, and a very, very solemn expression. We wanted her! She could be a good companion for Dodie.

We met Bob at the airport to welcome our new little girl. We learned that racially mixed children were treated horribly in her home country because they were of mixed races. But In Ai Lee nestled quickly into Roy's arms when he took her.

Again it would take time. Initially Debbie, as we had decided to call her, looked at people with an uninterested expression that never changed. No one could make her smile. Dodie and she looked each other over in sullen silence, with inscrutable eyes. A balloon changed that. At the studio set we had stopped off at on the way home a man gave her a balloon, and Debbie grinned as wide as the Mississippi River. She could smile!

In time Debbie learned to sleep in a bed, and not on the floor, as she had in Korea. She knew very few words of English when she came, and our communication was limited until the day she suddenly stopped speaking Korean and burst forth in fluent English.

Life priorities, family priorities. The Master Potter was shaping us for a truly unique ministry. But He also helped us to gain a new priority in our entertaining. Although Roy and I had always insisted on being part of clean entertainment, giving our life to the Master Potter changed that focus for us as well. We decided to add a "God and Country" number to our program, a song that was clearly inspirational and expressed our faith while not being overbearing in its message.

A major network asked us to do a variety show. They told us we could do whatever we wanted on it; they would not question what we did. We did the first show of the thirteen-week series at the Seattle World's Fair. It was beautiful, with "How Great Thou Art" as our closing number. The Ralph Carmichael orchestra performed with an incredibly blue sky with billowing clouds as background.

Taking a Stand

After the dress rehearsal the phone call from the network in New York fairly sizzled. Art Rush, our manager, got the call. He came and said to us, "You're going to have to take the word *Christ* out of the song. New York says it has to come out."

I said, "I am not deleting *Christ*. I am not doing it! Sorry. Tell them that. That's like tampering with 'Rock of Ages.'"

We left it in. But it really set us off on the wrong note with the network. So on every show that was just a little long they would try to chop out the Christian bit in the closing, but Roy would adamantly refuse to let them do it. When our thirteen weeks were up, they refused to renew our option for another thirteen weeks.

We had a similar experience in New York's Madison Square Garden. I'll let Roy tell what happened there:

"In that show I had a spot where I blacked out the turf and then threw a cross with lights on it while I sang 'Peace in the Valley.' The head of Madison Square Garden came into the dressing room and said, 'You can't put that cross in here. We have a lot of Jewish people here.'

"I said, 'We're not preaching. We're just telling how we feel. It's in the song, and we thought it would be effective.'

"He responded, 'We don't think you should put it in there.'

"I said, 'Well, either we put it in there, or we go home. If you don't want to use our show, we'll go home.'

"Grudgingly the manager said, 'Well, go ahead and try it.'

"Half of the Catholics in New York must have shown up for that matinee. When the cross hit the floor, they nearly tore the house down. So then they said to leave it in."

Making the Master our first priority let us experience some of the persecution Christians who give Him first place have always had. Look what the Lord paid for our salvation. For me the cost was never too much. We also discovered that the Master Potter was not only shaping us—He also took care of us.

Priorities. Before I gave myself wholeheartedly to the Master Potter, my priority was achieving my goals. Yet nothing ever quite satisfied me. It seemed like I was always not doing what I should do and doing what I shouldn't do. That all changed when Jesus Christ changed my priorities to living for Him, doing His will. And the rewards over the past forty-six years have been incredible. But that's for another chapter, where I'll let you see what happened with the children God entrusted to our care. Absolutely amazing!

We've briefly hinted at what the changed priorities meant for my professional ambitions. In the next chapter we'll look at how letting the Master Potter take over can change our personal ambitions.

Reflecting on the Shaping

1. Using the reshaping of priorities in the apostle Paul's life as an example, what priorities have been, or need to be, changed in your life?

2. In what area have you resisted the priorities you know the Master Potter is setting for you?

3. If you were to treat your spouse as a higher priority, how might it change your relationship?

4. If you love children and are childless, how might the Master Potter want to change your priorities?

5. How can you show your priorities as a believer in your work environment?

8

THE RESHAPING OF
PERSONAL AMBITION

What is it about ambition that has given it a bad
name? Is being ambitious bad in itself? Or is only
overweening ambition bad? Or should we also consider lack of focused ambition bad?

Can the Master Potter use only those who have no
real ambition in life, who perhaps will be totally submitted to Him? Will He remove ambition when the
new nature, energized by the Holy Spirit, takes over?
Or does He reshape ambition so it becomes part of the
"us" that God wants to use to His glory?

Consider the example of Lydia, the businesswoman the apostle Paul met outside the city gate of
Philippi. She is identified as a member of a group of
God-worshipers who had gathered on the banks of a
river. There she sat in the small circle, listening in-
tently as Paul talked with them about Jesus, the Messiah. Lydia quickly concluded that this made sense; as
Luke puts it, "the Lord opened her heart." She and the
members of her household believed the message of
new life in Christ and were baptized.

Now, Lydia was no fly-by-night businesswoman.

No discount store featuring leftover cloth for her. The Bible says she was a seller of purple cloth from Thyatira, the most expensive cloth on the market. She had not made her mark sitting at home and merely plying her needle or weaving cloth. She went where there was a market for purple, or royal, cloth—Philippi, a Roman city in what we today call Greece. She was clearly an ambitious woman.

As a result of her ambitious pursuit of her business, Lydia had become a wealthy woman. She had a household of servants, who clearly were extremely loyal to her. They all joined her in making a commitment to Jesus Christ.

Personal Ambition Reshaped

Lydia's first act as a new believer in Jesus Christ was to invite the apostle Paul and those who accompanied him into her home. The invitation was accepted, and he seems to have made her home his base for ministry in that city.

This ministry includes Paul's driving out the demonic spirit in the woman following them. Luke describes Paul and Silas being beaten and thrown into jail, where an earthquake opened all the doors. He portrays the terror of the jailer, who thought all the prisoners had escaped, but also the conversion of the jailer once he had heard the message of God's forgiveness.

Paul clearly stayed the night in the jailer's home. The magistrates, apparently before they heard of the earthquake and potential jailbreak, sent an early morning message to the jailer to release Paul and Silas. Paul decided to stand on his rights as a Roman citizen, so he let the magistrates know they had made a big mistake in the Roman world, beating a Roman citizen, and from his perspective a secret release would have gotten them off too lightly. Red-faced and apologetic magistrates were forced to publicly accompany Paul and Silas from prison.

Where did Paul and Silas go? To the home of Lydia, the lady who had given them hospitality before they were imprisoned.

Strangely, even though Paul mentions numerous women in his various letters, he never mentions Lydia. Did she go back to Thyatira to share the gospel in her home community? Did she take ill and die? We really don't know.

We can, it seems to me, make two deductions, based on circumstantial evidence. We do know that Paul told the Philippians that in the early months of his travels in Macedonia, they had been more generous in sharing with him financially than any other church. He wrote: "Now you Philippians know also that in the beginning of the gospel, when I departed from Macedonia, no church shared with me concerning giving and receiving but you only" (Phil. 4:15).

My guess is that Lydia was responsible for that. The ambitious, money-driven seller of purple had her ambition shaped by the Master Potter. Now she was helping others so they could share the gospel freely— especially the apostle Paul, who had brought her the message of new life in Christ.

A second deduction may be made from the last book of the Bible. In the book of Revelation, the apostle John is told to write messages to seven churches. There on the list of seven churches is Thyatira. Is it possible that Lydia, the seller of purple, returned to her home city and began sharing her newfound faith in Jesus Christ? That her family may have been responsible for founding the church mentioned in Revelation? Ambition redirected is a powerful force for good, it would appear, if we are reading the story of Lydia right.

I know a few things about ambition, as you have realized by now. As I reached adulthood, my ambition resulted in a two-decade battle for recognition as an entertainer. I fought for money, billing, and applause. I winced when ovations for others eclipsed mine. As an outspoken, aggressive woman, I found it hard to let anyone take credit for anything I thought belonged to me—especially when a man took the credit.

I guess you could say I was born ambitious. As a little girl I wanted to be a dancer, a ballerina, an entertainer—anything but what my parents wanted me to be, a schoolteacher. I saw elopement with my boyfriend as my escape route. His departure and our divorce put a temporary hold on my ambitions, but when my mother, my son Tom, and I moved to Memphis, my ambitions rekindled.

I was accepted at a business school even though I had not finished my junior year in high school. After business school an insurance company hired me as secretary, but I was more interested in show business than in the insurance business. My job gave me the income to do what I really wanted to do: establish myself as an entertainer.

Thwarted Ambitions

Off the job, I spent a great deal of time singing and accompanying myself on the piano. Initially I wrote short stories, but they only produced a parade of rejection slips. So I tried writing songs. Finally I wrote one that I thought was good enough to submit to a music publisher. I submitted it in person, sang it in the publisher's office, and was flattered by a vague promise that they would consider it. I waited for several months, then one day when I was in a music store I saw my tune, slightly altered, on sheet music bearing the name of another composer. I was devastated.

One day I was staring vaguely at an accident claim form in my typewriter. In reality, I was trying to come up with words for a tune I had just composed. My boss walked in, stood looking at me for a moment, and exploded, "Young lady, I think you are in the wrong business!" My fingers flew to the keyboard, and I typed like a maniac. He walked away, turned back, and asked, smiling, "How would you like to sing on a radio program?"

I was on cloud nine. I was about to step on the first rung of my ambitious ladder to the top in entertainment. The next Friday night Frances Fox made her radio debut, singing "Mighty Lak a Rose." I dedicated my song to my son, Tom. Someone must have liked it, for I was offered a regular spot in programming at the radio station.

Although singing on the radio provided no income, the exposure further fueled my ambition to be an entertainer. I was soon invited to sing at luncheons and banquets of civic organizations in town. Once in a while I got paid in real money; mostly I was paid in chicken croquettes and peas. But the experience was good, and soon I moved up to the most powerful radio station in Memphis.

Ambition, but No Common Sense

Ambition overcame common sense. As I became more popular I decided that if I could conquer Memphis, I could crack Chicago. But I did not crack Chicago—it broke me. After a few short years I wound up with a case of severe anemia due to overwork as a secretary. My parents had moved back to a farm in Texas, so I wired for money to go home. We were a miserable pair, Tom and I, as we rode the train to Texas, and I entered the hospital for two weeks of treatment with iron.

Three more months of rest fired up the old ambition. In the fall of that year I landed a good-paying job at radio station WHAS, where the program director gave me the name Dale Evans. It was designed primarily for ease of pronunciation for radio announcers—it is almost impossible to mispronounce or misspell.

That's where God made a serious attempt to redirect my ambition, when He let Tom become seriously ill with what even the doctors thought was polio, so I made lots of commitments to God as I walked and prayed in the halls of the hospital.

Ambition Stronger Than Spiritual Devotion

But my musical ambition was too strong, stronger than my spiritual devotion. This time I found a job as singer on the staff of radio station WFAA in Dallas. One day I had a phone call from a pianist and orchestral arranger I had dated frequently in Louisville. He said he was on his way to California to seek his fortune, and he wanted to stop in Dallas to see me. He stopped, was given a job with WFAA, and one year later we were married.

Ambition took over again two years later, so we moved to Chicago, where I landed a job as vocalist at the Balinese Room at the Blackstone Hotel. Later I was given a job as a jazz singer at the Edgewater Beach Hotel. But ballad singers were more popular than jazz vocalists, so I kept looking. I got on with the Anson Week's Orchestra, which played at the Aragon Ballroom, but also did one-nighters hundreds of miles apart. My schedule became too hectic for me.

By this time Tom was entering junior high school, and I wanted him with me. I auditioned for a job at WBBM, a CBS network station, and got it. I also sang at the Sherman and Drake hotels. I knew I was going places when I made it to the top spot, the then famous Chez Paree Supper Club.

Now that I had Tom with me I was again going to church regularly. I wanted him to have what I would not accept for myself—a solid relationship with the Lord. Every so often the minister would speak on the "claims of Christ," but I wanted nothing to do with them, suspecting they would interfere with my ambition. I told myself that my motivation was to guarantee a good future for Tom, helping him to go to college. He clearly had inherited my musical bent and would benefit from special training.

My real ambition during these years was to get into musical comedy in New York. My lack of dancing skills prevented that from happening when I was invited to join a Broadway show. But that ambition did not die.

Ambition and Compromise

Thus I laughed long and loud when I received a telegram from a Hollywood agent. He had heard me sing on a broadcast that reached California and asked for photographs of me. I considered this a real laugh, since I was convinced I was not pretty enough for the movies. On top of that, I was twenty-eight years old— too old, I thought, to begin in Hollywood. So I ignored the telegrams, but they kept on coming.

I finally took the telegrams to the program director at the radio station, who said I should give it a whirl. Still laughing, I took the inevitable glamour photos and sent them to the agent. He wired me to take a plane immediately for a screen test at Paramount Pictures.

My agent put me through a whirlwind of beauty preparations for my screen test. When I was asked about my age, my agent shouted, "Twenty-one." The day of the test I was carefully made up and gowned. As I sat there waiting for the crew to set up the lights, a sense of doubt and shame swept over me. I felt as though I would blow up because I was basically against deception, and my age was being misrepresented. Ambition was coming up against the biblical principles I had gained at home and in church, even though I still rejected the claims of the Master Potter on my life.

I walked over to my agent and told him I needed to talk to him. We walked out into the alley behind the studio and I said, "I have not been honest with you. I cannot go on with this thing until you know the facts. I am not twenty-one; I am twenty-eight. I have a son who is twelve years old. He lives with me."

His jaw dropped. He muttered, "Let me think, let me think." Suddenly he said, "You will have to send him away to school." I refused, saying that if Tom could not come to Hollywood with me, I would stay in Chicago. By this time the agent had invested too much effort and money in me to give up easily, so he tried another tack, "Tom is your brother. Do you understand?"

I still did not like it, but it gave me a chance to have Tom with me in Hollywood. So I said, "It's all right with me, if it's all right with Tom."

Tom responded, "It sounds pretty silly, but you can do anything you want, as long as I myself don't have to lie."

I figured if what I could make on a Hollywood job would send Tom to college and give him the musical education he so desperately wanted, that would help me achieve my ambition for my son. So I put aside my feelings of guilt and let my ambition take the reins.

Although Paramount did not take me, I did get on with Twentieth-Century Fox for a year at $400 per week, a princely sum compared to what I was getting in Chicago. We moved to West Los Angeles, rented a house large enough to include my husband's parents, and I prepared for another screen test. The first picture I was to be in was shelved because of Pearl Harbor. I started drama lessons, waiting for the next break.

Tom disappeared when there was any movie publicity work going on around the house. He told me again that he could never lie as I was lying, even for his own mother. He couldn't, he said, because he was a Christian, and Christians don't lie. That stung, but my ambition was strong enough to smother the lie and the guilt. I rationalized that I was doing it for him, for his future. I loved him and was proud of his natural musical ability. After a year at Twentieth-Century Fox I had had two bit parts in movies. I had also participated in a lot of shows for the boys in the Army camps. Then just before my contract was up, my agent joined the Air Force. Sure enough, I learned the studio would not renew my contract. Desperate, I called my agent and asked him to recommend someone who would get me back onto radio. He recommended Art Rush, whom I discovered was totally engrossed in working with a cowboy singer named Roy Rogers. All he could talk about was Roy.

Ambition and Moral Compromise

Art did get me an audition with NBC's "The Chase and Sanborn Hour," and I was hired. Everything seemed to be okay until I turned down the invitation to have dinner with a top executive in New York. Beginners usually accepted such invitations, but I told him I had a previous engagement with an old friend in the music publishing business. God was shaping my future and changing my ambition through the moral values I had gained at home and through my Bible reading and church attendance. I was not ambitious enough to totally reject my Christian values by having dinner with him; I was married.

The executive turned cold as ice. He eventually thawed enough to give me another chance—and another invitation to lunch. Again I turned him down. He took my turndowns as a personal insult, I discovered. The following fall I found myself replaced after the fourth show, with no hope of getting another commercially sponsored program for that season.

God kept providing opportunities for me to come to terms with my ambition—and let Him begin shaping it. My husband, Tom, and I attended First Baptist Church of Hollywood, where the pastor was what I call an "upsetter." Dr. Harold Proppe, it seemed to me, threw spiritual "shoes" at me, daring me to put them on. I kidded myself into thinking that I couldn't follow Him all the way now. Someday, when I was really safe and secure and ready to retire with enough money, I would give more time to Him and His work. I was furious one Sunday when Dr. Proppe suggested that people who had God-given talents in music and refused to honor God's house by using them there were disobedient. I just knew he was aiming right at me. I thought to myself, "Brother, if you only knew how demanding show business is, you wouldn't say that. I'm lucky to be here once a week."

Ambition Destroys Marriage

Ambition took its toll on my marriage as well. My husband worked evenings; I was up before dawn and ready for bed when he left. Although he did accompany me on the piano as often as he could when I sang at military bases, our opposite schedules drove us apart. In Hollywood, schedules are not made for the convenience of man and wife and children. You go where you have to go and do what you have to do, and married bliss can wait. We were making money, but the marriage did not last. I tasted the bitterness of another failure in marriage.

My shift to Art Rush brought another person with

Christian convictions into my life. Art had planned to go into the ministry, but halfway through a Christian college he decided against that and changed his degree. That did not dampen his faith or destroy the effects of an early Christian training. He never lost his love for God and the Bible. We talked a great deal about the Bible when we were together, and how he was trying to apply its laws to his life and work. This impressed me greatly.

At the same time I became really upset over Art's preoccupation with his big client, Roy Rogers. So I left him and signed up with Danny Winkler, who got me a year's contract with Republic Studios. In two weeks I was in a country musical called *Swing Your Partner*. At the end of the year Republic picked up my option.

My first picture was a western with a treatment similar to *Oklahoma* on Broadway. I gasped when I was told that the picture would star Roy Rogers. I hesitated, mumbling something about my ambition to get into a big sophisticated musical, and that I had never thought of doing westerns. Still, my heart reminded me that I had loved westerns ever since I was a kid in Texas—had *always* loved cowpokes and horses, as a good Texan should. But my whole theatrical ambition had been on the musical comedy side. On top of that, I had not been on a horse since the age of seven.

Ambition Goes Western

But God knew what He was about: He was shaping my ambition so I would fit into the plan He had for me with Roy Rogers and our international family. Despite a crash course in learning to ride and being saved from serious injury by quick action by Roy when my horse bolted, that first picture was a success. Eight films later I knew I was typecast—for good, it seemed. I tried to get out by leaving Republic Pictures, but failed to go anywhere and was invited back.

God shaped my ambition even more dramatically after I married Roy Rogers, beginning with the experience with the Master Potter as a result of Jack MacArthur's sermon. Republic Pictures' dismissal of me after marrying Roy had already changed my ambition from being a star in the movies to being a super mom to Roy's children. That new ambition became sharply focused after I gave my life totally over to the Master Potter less than two months after our marriage.

How do I know? Not long after both Roy and I had gone forward to commit our lives to Jesus Christ, my agent called to ask if I would like to do the leading role in the London company of *Annie Get Your Gun*. A year or so earlier I would have jumped at the opportunity. This was the big show toward which I had been pointing all my life. Yet it was clear to me now that I would work with Roy if I worked at all. As a result, Art Rush and I bought back my contract from Danny Winkler so that Art could be the agent for both Roy and me, even though I felt foolish doing it after ditching Art earlier.

Did this reshaping of ambition take me out of entertainment? Let me ask a parallel question. Did the Lord's reshaping of the apostle Paul's ambition after his Damascus road experience change his commitment to public ministry? Did Luke forget that he was a trained doctor after becoming the historian on the apostle Paul's team? No, in all three instances. My greatest fear as a youth had been that God would send me to Africa as a missionary; instead he let Roy and me become His ambassadors to the world through our television ministry, our testimonies at Billy Graham crusades, and our personal appearances.

Ambition and the Family

That does not mean that I recognized that after I committed my life to Christ. At that point I had just assumed the role of stepmother to Roy's three children, and I was quite prepared to let being a wife and mother be my role for some years. I felt I had missed out on raising Tom, since I had him with me only sporadically, and he had really been raised by my mother.

I sorely missed being part of my son's toddling years, seeing him play in his first ballgame, being the one to personally buy his first "knee-pant suit." I was working in an office (of necessity because of my failed marriage), struggling to get into show business (not of necessity) during those years. I remember how I cried over my little boy's absence when I left him with my mother and traveled to Chicago to try to break into show business. I was determined not to make the same mistake twice, giving my career first place because of ambition.

The wife of a friend, on the other hand, let the Lord shape her ambition during her children's crucial formative years. Although she had worked part-time in radio drama in Chicago, she had also been a vocal soloist in oratorio since fourteen. When she entered a music festival in Chicago while her children were still preschoolers, she placed second and was invited to become the student of the leading opera coach in the city. Months later the artistic director of the Chicago Lyric Opera asked her to join the opera company in a new production.

Imagine the surprise of the vocal coach and the artistic director when she replied, "I'm sorry, but I cannot take on such a demanding role now. I have seen too many musicians divorce because they had no time left for their spouses. My husband and two children are more important than a career in opera at this time."

She continued to sing in her church and as soloist in oratorio, but she was also involved as choir leader. When her daughter was in college and her son in his junior year in high school, she agreed to teach music part-time in a Christian day school. Twenty years after turning down the opportunity in Chicago she auditioned for a regional opera company—and embarked on seven years of growing success. Now she could help ambitious young people come to terms with their insecurities and relationship problems.

When asked if she ever regretted turning down the plum role she was offered, she replies, "Never! Not when I see what the Lord has done in our children's lives—and what He has done in our marriage." Now she is rejoicing in her role as grandmother, with both son and daughter happily married, singing to two lovely granddaughters.

Looking back on my experience of being a multiethnic, multicultural family I say, "Right on!" At this stage sixteen grandchildren and twenty-seven great-grandchildren make me so thankful I took the time to be a mother rather than just fulfilling my ambition to be a superstar entertainer. The many trips we took as a family during the summers, and the opportunities the children had to participate in the shows cemented us as a family. Fulfilling my ambition to have a large family proved far more satisfying than being a lead singer or a leading lady in westerns.

Refocused Ambition

Here's how the apostle Paul expressed his reshaped ambition:

> *I have been crucified with Christ; it is no longer I*
> *who live, but Christ lives in me; and the life which I*
> *now live in the flesh I live by faith in the Son of*
> *God, who loved me and gave Himself for me. (Gal.*
> *2:20)*

In writing to the Philippians he puts it a little differently, but with the same focus:

> *Yet indeed I also count all things loss for the*
> *excellence of the knowledge of Christ Jesus my*
> *Lord, for whom I have suffered the loss of all things,*
> *and count them as rubbish . . . that I may know*
> *Him and the power of His resurrection, and the*
> *fellowship of His sufferings, being conformed to His*
> *death, if, by any means, I may attain to the*
> *resurrection from the dead. (Phil. 3:8, 10–11)*

Once I gained that focus on becoming like Christ, being His ambassador, achieving His plans for my life, my personal ambition was indeed changed. The Master Potter now was able to continue shaping it to suit His purposes throughout the forty-six years since then. Not that I was ever perfect, just as the apostle

Paul insists he did not reach perfection on earth, but I knew what I was here for—to serve the Master Potter with all the talents and abilities He has given me. We'll get into that a little more in the next chapter.

Reflecting on the Shaping

1. Why do you think Lydia of Thyatira was so ready to have her ambition reshaped when she heard the message of life in Christ from the apostle Paul?

2. What escape routes have you taken to attempt to fulfill your own ambition?

3. What compromises have you faced as you have attempted to fulfill your ambition?

4. If you are a young mother, has the Lord been talking to you about personal ambition? Could you put it on hold until the children are older so the Master Potter can shape your mothering role?

5. What is God saying to you about priorities as you read Philippians 3:8–11?

9

THE RESHAPING OF ABILITIES

You may be asking, "When you accepted the shaping of the Master Potter, did He enhance your abilities? Did He change your abilities? Did He give you a larger platform on which to perform with the abilities He gave you?"

I cannot say I was a better singer or a better actress. But I certainly had incredible inner peace, and that changed the way I performed.

During the twenty years I was an entertainer on radio and in westerns I never lost my fear of going on stage in public appearances. I always worried sick about how I would perform, be accepted. I'd have to say that for all my bravado, I was basically an insecure entertainer.

Then I committed my life to the Master Potter. I remember the first time after my commitment to Him that I was asked to sing in front of a church audience. Our church had a radio ministry every Sunday afternoon, and I was glad to go on the air for them. When I felt the fright coming on, I stopped and prayed that God would work through me, that I would feel within myself that He was speaking and singing through me as His agent. The sense of relaxation and freedom that came over me is indescribable. I felt no fear, no nervousness whatsoever.

I had little time to rehearse for that program. Some of the roles I played were far more difficult than anything I had done before. I was amazed at what came out of me when I listened to the rebroadcasts. Obviously we become more effective communicators when we are no longer controlled by fear; so you might say the Master Potter enhanced my ability to communicate in song.

Enhanced Ability

Remember Peter, the Galilean fisherman? He left his nets to follow Jesus, but when Jesus sent the disciples to Galilee, telling them that He would meet them there, Peter went back to fishing. That's what he had honed his skills on before Jesus called him. When Jesus appeared on the shore after His resurrection, this highly experienced fisherman had to admit that they had fished all night and caught nothing. So then Jesus, the ex-carpenter, said: "Cast the net on the right side of the boat, and you will find some" (John 21:6).

The result of obedience? "So they cast, and now they were not able to draw it in because of the multitude of fish" (John 21:6).

I have been truly astonished what people have been able to accomplish when they put themselves unreservedly under the hand of the Master Potter.

Or think of Dr. Luke, who left his practice to become the apostle Paul's traveling companion and witness for Jesus Christ. Did God ditch Dr. Luke's training and abilities and simply turn him into a positive witness for Jesus Christ? On the contrary, God used his medical knowledge to help keep the apostle Paul on the road despite incredibly difficult traveling conditions.

More than that, when you read the Gospel of Luke and the book of Acts, you will, if you look, find him making detailed notes of the medical conditions of people who approached Jesus. Luke's writings are genuine repositories of medical information from that day, reflecting his training. It is Dr. Luke who provides the stories of the healing of Peter's mother-in-law (Luke 4:38), a leper (5:12), a paralyzed man (5:18), and a deformed hand (6:6).

Reshaped Abilities

So when Luke committed himself to the Master Potter, He not only reshaped Luke's abilities by turning him into a historian, but He also used Luke's knowledge of medicine in ministry outreach.

Similarly, the Master Potter did not cast aside my abilities when He took over. Although Republic Studios initially brought in another leading lady to star in the movies opposite Roy after our marriage, fans of Roy soon let management know this was a mistake. So I was invited to rejoin Roy in the movies and continue to use my already-developed abilities. But that did not last long.

Roy had been with Republic Studios for fourteen years, starring in about ninety movies. About a year after Robin's birth, his contract was up for renewal. By this time, television was gaining strength and had to be factored into Roy's future. So he told the head of

Republic Studios that he would sign only if he had television privileges. Mr. Yates hit the roof, for the moviemakers of the day were still fighting television. Roy refused to budge, insisting on television rights.

Mr. Yates adamantly refused, but Roy moved into television despite him, where he and I could work together. The Master Potter was moving both of us into a whole new use of our abilities, for now we were in control of our programming and could tailor the message we wanted to communicate. We now were also able to develop our own shows for the rodeo circuit and major cities as well.

Latent Abilities Reshaped

God not only reshaped our opportunities in entertainment, but He also gave me success in a totally unexpected arena. You'll remember that I had fancied myself a short story writer while still in my teens, but I had seen only rejection slips. But when God took us through the major reshaping of our priorities, of our focus on what is important through Robin, He also reshaped my abilities as a writer.

Amazingly, God used another negative experience to begin that reshaping. The day after Robin's funeral, feeling like I was on the ragged edge of a nervous breakdown, I was sitting in the kitchen, trying to regroup. The back door burst open and two strange women walked in. One of them said, "Mrs. Rogers, I know this is a bad time to come to your house, right after your baby's death, but my aunt is here from the East and she simply has to meet you and your husband and see your house before she goes back."

I was stunned at their audacity. Were we celebrities to be gawked at like three-legged calves or baubles in a jeweler's window? I dabbed my eyes with a napkin and said as civilly as I could, "You are right; this is not the time to see our home, and I'm not up to showing it to you. Roy is in the den, if you want to see him." They pushed past me into the den. What Roy said, I never bothered to ask, but they rushed out of the house in too much of a hurry to say good-bye.

The next day I was thinking of Robin's death, the uncivil intrusion, and its implications. I looked up at an etching of Robin and recalled Roy's words, "She looks like a small-size sleeping angel." Suddenly the Holy Spirit reminded me of Hebrews 13:2: "Be not forgetful to entertain strangers: for thereby some have entertained angels unawares" (KJV).

Like the sun breaking through the clouds, it became clear to me that Robin had been a little ministering angel to our family, teaching us badly needed lessons about the true values of life. Her handicaps were the Master Potter's audiovisual lessons to teach us that the strength of the Lord is made perfect in weakness. For two years she had been the Master Potter's instrument to teach us humility, patience, gratitude to God for what He has given us, and dependence upon God.

Impulsively I reached out for a pen and began to write. I wrote so quickly that after an hour my hand began to cramp. I stopped and looked down in disbelief at the little pile of paper on the desk. I couldn't believe I had written so much so quickly.

Some days later, while Roy and I were on a radio broadcast, I was able to rest for a few moments away from the mike. I closed my eyes and began to pray

about Robin's message. I suddenly felt strongly
moved again to write her story.

For weeks I couldn't shake the urging I felt. As I
wrote, Robin's story poured forth. I really believe God
gave me the words to write. I kept a tablet and a
pencil handy and jotted down notes and thoughts as
they came to me. If no tablet was handy, I made notes
on the backs of envelopes, script sheets, the margins
of newspapers. Three months later the book, Robin
and God's book, was finished. Mine was the hand that
the Master Potter used.

We left for appearances in New York via Dallas,
where, as I shared earlier, we visited Hope Cottage
and adopted Dodie. The press conferences and appearances in New York were extremely rough. I was
still so emotionally upset over Robin's death that I
could not make sense to anyone. I would pray every
step of the way from our dressing rooms to the chutes,
and during the show asked God to steady me as Roy
and I shook hands with the children in the stands, as
we always did at the end of our show. Each night I
made it, dry-eyed, back to the hotel.

After ten days I was an emotional wreck. I had
slept little, and when I did I had nightmares in which
I saw Robin in her casket, sitting up and looking at me
with questioning eyes. I would wake up crying and
try to pray. I felt my prayers went no higher than the
ceiling.

I began to wonder if Robin had been just a mistake of
nature, if God really knew or cared. I questioned
whether the book I had been guided to write was simply
my desire to get an affliction off my chest, after hiding
Robin's Down's syndrome condition from the public for
two years.

The tenth morning, hollow-eyed and shaking from shattered nerves, I said to Roy, "I'm going out in Central Park and sit there on a bench until God tells me something. I can't go on like this. I just have to have some rest and assurance that He is directing me with Robin's book. He simply has to help me."

I took my Bible and walked out into the lovely autumn sunshine to a stone bench near the Central Park Zoo. I bowed my head and prayed, "Thy will be done, Lord. Not my will, but Thine! But—*please* give me a word. Please give me peace about Robin and her book. Is it Your will that I seek a publisher for it? Will it help Your cause? Will it help children like Robin— and their parents? *Please.*"

I looked up after that prayer. Walking toward me was a little Down's syndrome girl about six years old, holding the hand of a middle-aged woman whose face showed the scars of mental anguish. The child had all the characteristics of Down's syndrome: the slanted eyes, weak and out of control; tiny ears and little square hands; thick tongue, drooling; the unsteady, labored walk.

There were hundreds of people in the park walking in the noon sunshine, but I really did not see them. I only saw that child walking toward me. Suddenly it hit me. I had asked God for a word, and He had sent it in this child. *He had spoken to me!* He was saying, "I have taken Robin so that you can speak of Me to children like this, and to mothers like this. Robin is safe in the Everlasting Arms. Now tell others how she has blessed your life in giving you an awareness of Me, and how all the other Down's syndrome children in the world can bless all these other mothers."

I fairly ran back through the park to the hotel

room, burst into our suite, and shouted to Roy, "He did it! God did it! He spoke to me!"

God's Ally

As though guided by God's hand, I picked up the phone and called Marble Collegiate Church and asked for an appointment with Dr. Norman Vincent Peale, who had written the book that had helped me so much, *A Guide to Confident Living*. From the secretary I got the answer I had expected: Dr. Peale was a very busy man with a tight schedule. People made appointments weeks ahead of time, and she rather doubted I could see him. But she would check and see. She checked, and God opened the door. Fifteen minutes later I walked into his office.

"Dr. Peale, I have written a little book about my baby. May I read just a little of it to you?"

Famous last words—how many writers have said the same thing to authors who are successful!

"Of course," Dr. Peale said gently. "But first, we'll pray."

We prayed—on our knees. I got a tight hold on my emotions, fought back tears, and read what God had given me. Then I looked up at him; he had not said a word during the reading. I was almost afraid I was boring him. He returned my look through glistening eyes and said, "It's beautiful! I will help you get it published."

But I guess the Master Potter decided He had to teach me more about humility, trust, and dependence on Him. Dr. Peale's publisher already was launching a book about a little girl with cerebral palsy and so was not interested in my book.

Then Dr. Peale sent me to another publisher's office. They were very kind, but wary of my "presumption that the soul of a two-year-old should have such scope of spiritual understanding." They doubted that "God would talk that way to a baby—or the baby to God."

Two blows in a row! Yet after that Central Park experience I was not let down or discouraged. After this latest news had just sunk in, I had a call from Dr. Frank S. Mead, editor-in-chief at Fleming H. Revell. He had been in the publisher's office after I had left the building and wanted to read my manuscript on his way to Chicago on a business trip. Later he called from Chicago and said, "We want it!"

I wept—this time for joy. No more rejection letters; the Master Potter had reshaped my abilities to fit His purpose.

God Plus Abilities Equals Success

The next spring I had one of my periodic physical breakdowns from overwork. When I came home from the hospital I found a mountain of mail from people who were reading *Angel Unaware*. Revell released it just before Easter 1953, and in a short time it was on the best-seller list. I took a series of potent iron shots to stimulate my very low hemoglobin, and went at the mountain of mail.

When I realized that this book was a true best-seller, I started wondering about the royalties. Having written the book to help other little "Robins," I came to see that my royalties, as well as my energies, should go toward helping such children. A lot of money was needed for research and the publicity needed to acquaint the public with this desperate need. At the time I knew of no national organization specifically founded for such a purpose. I was at a loss just where to allocate the funds, so I prayed—and God answered.

About a month after the release of the book, Roy and I were doing a radio broadcast at NBC when we were approached by a man and two women. They wanted to take a publicity picture of us for use in a fund drive for the Exceptional Children's Foundation in Los Angeles. Exceptional children! I liked that. I liked it even better when they explained that this foundation was a branch of the National Association for Retarded Children. Started in 1950, the year Robin was born, the Association was headquartered in New York.

I was so overcome I could hardly speak. I immediately wrote to Revell and asked that they send all my royalties to the National Association for Retarded Children. *Angel Unaware* was on its way to helping many more children and parents than I had ever imagined possible. Today there is a school in Oklahoma called The Dale Rogers School for the Retarded. When the National Association for Retarded Children disbanded, I redirected the royalties to The Exceptional Children's Foundation in Los Angeles.

No Abortion Because of Angel Unaware

When the Master Potter reshapes our abilities, He can use them in truly amazing ways. More than one and a half million copies of *Angel Unaware* sold, and forty years later the book is still in print. I have met many people to whom this book ministered in very special ways.

Years later, a woman called with a story that touched me deeply. She had taken the drug thalidomide, and her doctors told her to abort her baby, since the child would be horribly deformed. Someone gave her a copy of *Angel Unaware*. After reading it, she decided she would trust God and have the baby.

This grateful mother called me because she wanted me to know that her little girl was born perfect. She thanked me for writing about our little Robin Elizabeth. The caller said, "If I had listened to all the frightening stories about abnormal children and gone through with the abortion, I would never have known the blessing of my beautiful little girl."

You'll remember my attempts at songwriting. When the Master Potter began reshaping my abilities, He gave me the song "The Bible Tells Me So" to use in one of our television episodes. Weeks later the song was featured on "Hit Parade," staying on it for many weeks. Later it was sung in churches and Sunday schools all over the country. When we put our abilities in the hands of the Master Potter, He uses them to lift up our heavenly Father, who gave them to us.

Joseph's Abilities Shaped

I think of Joseph, the young man so despised by his brothers that they sold him to slave traders on their way to Egypt. Out of sight, out of mind, was their idea. But the Master Potter took this super-confident young man and began shaping his abilities. First He placed him in the home of Potiphar, the highly placed Egyptian military officer, to learn how to manage a smaller household. Joseph did so well he became Potiphar's right-hand man—only to be falsely accused by Potiphar's wife.

Now notice that God begins reshaping his abilities in a new, less hospitable environment: prison. The Bible reports:

> *He gave him favor in the sight of the keeper of the prison. And the keeper of the prison committed to Joseph's hand all the prisoners who were in the prison; whatever they did there, it was his doing. The keeper of the prison did not look into anything that was under Joseph's authority, because the LORD was with him; and whatever he did, the LORD made it prosper. (Gen. 39:21–23)*

Undoubtedly the politics of running the household of Potiphar and then prison management prepared Joseph for his biggest assignment: chief executive under the pharaoh. His assignment: to make the results of seven fruitful years last through seven lean years. A nomadic herdsman had become the most powerful man in Egypt beneath the pharaoh because he had let the Master Potter shape his abilities.

I have seen God do that kind of shaping, though possibly not as dramatic, in our children's lives. A good example is my son, Tom, whom God used so miraculously to bring me to my knees at the Master Potter's feet. After graduating from the University of Southern California, he joined the Army for two years. He was so good as a musician that he was invited to join the prestigious Air Force Band, the best band in the services at the time. It was a plum as far as postings go, but he turned it down because he did not feel God wanted him there.

When he reentered civilian life, Tom became a music teacher in the public school system, staying at that for twenty-seven years, teaching both choral and instrumental music. But he also directed music in churches. After a teacher strike in his school district, the Lord led him out of public school teaching into becoming "teacher" of worship in a full-time position as Minister of Music at Arcade Baptist Church in Sacramento.

For years Tom and Barbara gave a month to serve the Lord in special ways as part of their vacation. One time they went to Mexico to build churches. Then when their oldest daughter and her husband went to Amsterdam with Youth With a Mission, Tom and Barbara went there each summer to do street evangelism. Tom would play his flute and Barbara the keyboard.

When Tom reached retirement age, a long-cherished dream of full-time mission service became possible. A music teacher at the Black Forest Academy in Germany, a high school for children of missionaries, had to take a year off for health reasons. She had directed choirs, but now the school wanted someone who could teach instrumental music and lead orchestras. Tom fit that description, so he and Barbara went there for a year.

Tom leads two orchestras and directs the choirs at the school. But he also plays the clarinet in the town band during their festivals. He and Barbara just fit right in. The Master Potter had reshaped their abilities over the years so they could serve under very demanding conditions.

Humility the Key

What does it take to have our abilities shaped and reshaped through the years to fit the Master Potter's purposes? I'm convinced the key quality is humility. Nowhere is this more evident than in a wife and mother's life while her children are still young. It is so easy to let the voices in today's feminist world convince young women that their abilities are grossly underused if they stay home to care for their children. Yet that is exactly where, I believe, the Master Potter wants to reshape our abilities—unless, of course, economic setbacks make taking a job necessary.

For one thing, the Master Potter loves to reshape a young mother's creativity, let it develop fully in interaction with her children. As God's gift, children deserve the best we can offer them—and the best is theirs only if we let the Master Potter shape us.

Creativity in the Home

For example, we can teach our children to talk with God in uninhibited fashion. When our children were living at home, we had a family altar (actually an old radio and television console). There I encouraged them to pray and tell Jesus about their problems, thanking Him for their blessings. The altar was the focal point of the living room.

I draped different coverings over this console, keeping in mind the season of the year. I had the girls pick flowers to brighten it. We had an antique New England kneeling bench, covered with petit point, in front of this makeshift altar. Sometimes I would kneel down beside the children. At other times I would respect their desire to be alone with the Lord. Our organ sat at the opposite side of the room. Next to it was a glass door leading to the patio. In one of the panels of the door we placed a lovely picture of Jesus. When the light shone through the door, it illuminated the picture and lit up the whole room.

I share this example only to stimulate young mothers to think creatively of ways to develop an environment of thanksgiving and prayer in their home. When you let the Master Potter reshape your abilities in the home, He can honor you with opportunities in the church and in the community. Once your children are old enough for you to consider entering the work force again, you will be ready to apply your sharpened abilities in that environment.

Remember my story of the woman who turned down an opportunity in opera? She first developed her abilities at home. Then she served as music director for three weeks in a Christian children's camp, and later served as program director in another camp. Then she was given an opportunity to lead a choir in a small church.

These opportunities honed her skills so that she was invited to teach music in a Christian grammar school with a strong academic record even though she did not have a degree in music. Later she led a large choir in major oratorio presentations. All of this provided the shaping needed for the day when she auditioned for, and won, roles in operas years later.

Humility Not Easy to Attain

Humility: the willingness to endure the shaping by the Master Potter when you think your abilities call for better opportunities. Since I am strictly an "up-front" person in my thinking and actions, humility has been hard for me. My background in show business rates this quality quite low on the scale. In this profession, performance is based on ego, selling one's personality, and relying on the words of the critics for self-evaluation. One is either up or down, according to the box office receipts, media ratings, or public opinion. This is one of the major reasons why the entertainment business is a hard row for the Christian to hoe and keep his or her eyes on the Lord.

How is the Master Potter at work shaping and reshaping your abilities? He really does have a plan for you, if you accept what the psalmist writes in Psalm 139:16:

> *Your eyes saw my substance,*
> *being yet unformed.*
> *And in Your book they all were written,*
> *The days fashioned for me,*
> *When as yet there were none of them.*

Clearly, the psalmist believed that the shaping you are now experiencing may have long-range goals you cannot even dream about yet. So why not give Him full rein now?

In the next chapter, we will consider one more facet in which the Master Potter is at work: reshaping your relationships.

Reflecting on the Shaping

1. How did the reshaping of ambitions affect Dale's

ability to communicate as a singer when she was asked to sing Christian songs?

2. What can we learn from the incident in John 21 about the potential results of obeying God, even when our obedience seems unlikely to produce anything?

3. Luke, author of several books in the New Testament as well as an associate of Paul's, was originally a physician, but when he met the Master Potter, he developed a new skill: that of being a missionary (and historian) for Christ. Have you experienced a similar development of a second skill as Luke did when he became a full-time witness?

4. What does Dale's experience in writing the book *Angel Unaware* mean in terms of how God might use you in ways you hadn't expected? Are you willing to take the risks associated with the Master Potter's reshaping of your abilities?

10

THE RESHAPING OF RELATIONSHIPS

*E*ven though after my first divorce I determined I would carve out my own future independent of anyone else, I discovered I needed relationships with others. I entered these relationships without seeking what God had in mind for me. As a result, problems with relationships haunted me for the two decades I refused to submit to the shaping of the Master Potter.

As long as I initiated relationships strictly on my own feelings, my likes and dislikes, my relationships with men in particular put me on an emotional roller coaster. Try as I might, I could not seem to get off it. Once I submitted to the Master Potter, He reshaped my priorities, my goals, and helped me develop the patience for relationships that could survive the intense public scrutiny and marriage pressures of a show business career.

Psychiatry is beginning to recognize what the Master Potter determined after He made humans. God said after He created Adam: "It is not good that the man should be alone; I will make him an help meet for him" (Gen. 2:18 KJV).

God did not create us to be independent, autonomous units in society. He created us to thrive in relationships in which we nurture and support each other as well as develop the mutual accountability that will foster both personal and relationship growth.

Allison Bass, in an article in the *Boston Globe* on May 19, 1993, reported that psychotherapists at Wellesley College's Stone Center developed a treatment approach that considered women's intense need for relationships as intrinsically healthy, rather than a form of psychological illness, which had been the prevailing attitude when treating abused women. When put into practice in a women's psychiatric unit at Boston's McLean Hospital, this new attitude in therapy proved remarkably effective. Helping women realize that their need for relationships was healthy and helping them work through their relationship traumas proved more effective than approaches that sought to help women overcome the need for relationships.

Families Start the Process

Adult relationships are not, however, shaped in a vacuum. God puts us into families to start the process—and mine was a genuinely caring extended family. I was an extrovert, but I was also extremely sensitive. I was fortunate enough to have relatives around me who understood that. I visited their homes many times during my childhood, for my brother was afflicted with more than his share of illnesses, and I was a handful that my mother must have been glad to be rid of as often as possible.

I idolized my Grandfather Wood. We spent every Christmas and part of every summer with him in

Uvalde, Texas. I sensed in him a rare spark of understanding and affection that added such richness to my life. He was old, but he never lost his youthfulness or his love for children and young people. I have no doubt that he was used by God as a role model to shape my love for children, making me eager to enlarge our family through adoption.

I suspect I acquired my strongly independent and non-conformist streak, but also my love for fun, from my great-grandfather. A crusty, unconventional, and completely lovable old rebel, Grandpa went his own way and stood on his own feet, no matter what. When his eyesight began to fail, he refused to be driven to prayer meetings on Wednesday nights. Employing a cane, he navigated his way to church in the middle of the village street, even though people laughed at him and were annoyed at his recklessness.

These relationships, and many others, all contributed to who I became. But I also recognize that misused, some of these qualities became destructive in my life. Only when the Master Potter began reshaping me could they become fit for His service and used to the glory of God.

Despite all the special treatment I received from my mother and aunts as a precocious little girl, my relationship problems started as soon I entered my teenage years and began testing my wings. I did not like the restrictions I felt my parents and our Baptist church put on my career goals.

My mother wanted me to finish high school and become a music teacher—I wanted to sing and dance my way to the top in the entertainment field. She wanted me to settle down nearby—I wanted to test what the world had to offer me. I did not realize that in that rebellion against my parents I was sowing the seeds for relationship disasters. I was too strong-headed to recognize the truth of the biblical principle: "Honor your father and your mother, that your days may be long upon the land which the LORD your God is giving you" (Ex. 20:12).

Consequences of Rebellion

Somehow the fact that this was emphasized in the New Testament as well by the apostle Paul in Ephesians 6:1–3 escaped me—or I was unwilling to accept it. As a result, I eloped at fourteen, completely oblivious to the consequences in store for me. Even when nothing turned out right in future relationships, I failed to recognize that it was God disciplining me. Instead of turning to God, I struck out in all directions, hurting myself and often hurting others. I constantly rationalized my growing sense of guilt, trying to justify my wrongdoing. I did not realize I needed to look to God for the only perfect love that is available to us in our marriage relationships.

In God's mercy and grace, He kept after me until I recognized that discarding an unsatisfactory relationship for a more promising one just kept me on the roller coaster. When I married Roy I was determined that this time it was for life, but that became a reality only because less than two months later I submitted to the Master Potter's reshaping of my relationship.

Guidelines from the Bible

I found that the Bible provides clear guidance for the cement that keeps a marriage together. In an earlier chapter we focused on Hannah and her desire for a child, which she felt was essential to cementing her relationship with her husband, Elkanah, and quieting her tormentor, Penninah. A frequently overlooked aspect of that relationship is Elkanah's support for Hannah despite her childlessness. He asks: "Hannah, why do you weep? Why do you not eat? And why is your heart grieved? Am I not better to you than ten sons?" (1 Sam. 1:8).

Some have interpreted this as the typical arrogance of a man who does not recognize the emotional needs of a woman. Although she has a loving husband, she cannot be emotionally satisfied without a child to love and care for.

That's a valuable insight, but it is also true that Elkanah demonstrated the kind of love needed to sustain a marriage relationship. Most men in Israel at that time determined a wife's value by whether she could bear a son, but Elkanah insisted that his love was not diminished by her barrenness. His love was, in fact, unconditional.

Love like that sets the tone for a marriage relationship since it expresses Christ's unconditional love for us. The kind of love the Master Potter has given us as Christians is described in Romans 5:5: "The love of God has been poured out in our hearts by the Holy Spirit who was given to us."

Then the apostle Paul describes the dimensions of this love, the self-sacrificing nature of the love the Holy Spirit has literally "poured out" in our hearts:

> *But God demonstrates His own love toward us, in*
> *that while we were still sinners, Christ died for us. . . .*
> *For if when we were enemies we were reconciled to*

God through the death of His Son, much more,
having been reconciled, we shall be saved by His
life. (Rom. 5:8, 10)

The Impact of Unconditional Love

How our recognition and acceptance of this great, unconditional love of Christ should affect our relationships, and certainly our marriage, is illustrated by the apostle Paul in Romans 15:7: "Therefore receive one another, just as Christ also received us, to the glory of God."

When I accepted the Master Potter's challenge to let Him reshape my relationships, that's the love He poured out into my heart for Roy and his children, and later for Robin and our adopted children.

Based on what I was learning about the reshaping of relationships, I recognized that, led by the Holy Spirit, I needed to attempt to repair broken relationships. My mother and I, for example, entered an entirely new level of relationship when I confessed my rebellion as sin and began sharing her joy in the Lord. She had always been supportive in taking care of Tom whenever I called on her, but she was also constantly saddened by my attempts to run my own life and achieve my own goals. Now our relationship could mature as we worshiped and served the Lord on the same wavelength.

I also set about making restitution wherever possible for past breakdowns in relationships. Despite my best efforts, it often proved impossible to make full and just restitution. I found it excruciatingly painful that I could not get rid of guilt even with my efforts at restitution. Only when I recognized that Christ died to relieve me of guilt, that He died to cover every sin through His atonement, did I gain relief.

No Marriage Breakdown Is Good

Don't let anyone tell you that the breakdown of a marriage relationship is ever good. It may appear to be the only alternative, but separation and divorce are never "good." The fact is that the ultimate breakdown of a relationship, a divorce, provides a taste of hell. No matter who is to blame, and each spouse is normally equal to blame, divorce can only be defined as a failure to fulfill a contract between two people. It demonstrates a failure on the part of both to extend unconditional love to the other partner in the relationship. In my experience, divorce was like losing a part of myself to death. I have experienced both divorce and the death of a child, and I'm convinced they are on a par as the two most devastating experiences in life. In fact, you can emotionally write *finis* to the death of a child, even though I used to see Robin in the face of many children. But you really never write *finis* to a divorce; the other person is alive, and often around, for years, especially if there are children. That sense of failure returns to haunt you with every contact and every sight of the name.

On top of that, I discovered that I carried the fears, hurts, and resentments of a previous broken relationship into the next marriage. This emotional baggage prevented a true fresh start and the adequate handling of new hurts and resentments. I was always looking for the Dream Prince to ride up in shining armor and sweep me away to endless love and contentment. I never quite realized I was no prize myself.

That's where the Master Potter performed His reshaping miracle in my life once I submitted my whole being to Him. As a result, Roy and I have been married for forty-six years, despite my earlier failures when I entered relationships on my own.

What a far cry from the easy in, easy out, attitude toward marriage today, where unconditional love is not even considered an important factor in the relationship.

The Master Potter is at work reshaping many other kinds of relationships as well. What is the goal of the Master Potter in this, and are any common attitudes and actions foundational for both marriage and other relationships? I believe the Master Potter has provided rather clear goals for His reshaping of attitudes and actions once we submit to His loving hands.

I've already indicated how important family relationships are as the Master Potter shapes us for what He ultimately has in mind for us. Naturally, these family relationships continue throughout life and can provide a lot of emotional and practical support. But all of us need the basic relationship with a friend as well—that is especially true for women, as I indicated at the beginning of this chapter.

Poignant Example of Friendship

A truly poignant example is the friendship of Jonathan, the son of King Saul, and David, who was Public Enemy No. 1 as far as King Saul was concerned. We read about their relationship: "When he [David] had finished speaking to Saul, the soul of Jonathan was knit to the soul of David, and Jonathan loved him as his own soul" (1 Sam. 18:1).

That relationship was kindled by the Master Potter in the hearts of both Jonathan and David and was nurtured by their admiration for each other, their trust in each other, and their willingness to sacrifice for each other. They cemented the relationship in a covenant, as we read in verse 3, with Jonathan taking off his royal robe and giving it, along with his armor and even his sword and his bow and his belt, to David. In effect, Jonathan was saying, "I trust you so much I am totally disarming myself and arming you. I know you will not turn on me but will use what I am giving you to fight the enemies of Israel."

That kind of trust is praiseworthy, but could it stand the test of time and the petty jealousies that arise in the king's court? As long as David kept beating up on the Philistines he remained in King Saul's good graces. But when King Saul "saw that he [David] behaved very wisely, he was afraid of him" (1 Sam. 18:15). King Saul began to see David as a rival instead of a key leader in his army, and he turned against David.

Now comes the emotional struggle the son of a king must have had when his father turns against his best friend. Jonathan agreed to determine his father's true motives toward David. When David was absent from his usual place in court for several days, King Saul became suspicious. He interrogated Jonathan, who provided the excuse that David had gone to make sacrifices with his family in Bethlehem.

King Saul gradually realized that there was more to it than that. He accused Jonathan:

"You son of a perverse, rebellious woman! Do I not know that you have chosen the son of Jesse to your

*own shame and to the shame of your mother's
nakedness? For as long as the son of Jesse lives on
the earth, you shall not be established, nor your
kingdom. Now therefore, send and bring him to me,
for he shall surely die." (1 Sam. 20:30–31)*

Relationships That Risk It All

Jonathan's relationship with David was so deep he
really was not concerned about his own future. So he
risked his life, knowing how temperamental his father
had become, by asking, "Why should he be killed?
What has he done?" King Saul, who by now had become irrational because of his insane jealousy of
David, threw his spear at Jonathan to kill him.

Jonathan secretly met with David to inform him
that King Saul was determined to kill David. Again,
Jonathan and David expressed their commitment to
each other. They confirmed the covenant they had
made about David's taking care of Jonathan's family if
anything should happen to him.

Too ideal a story to be true? Just another priestly
story to generate heroic loyalty among young men as
they fought for their country?

Hardly, for David did care for Jonathan's family,
because the Master Potter had "poured out" an unconditional love in David's heart. We also have a New
Testament example, for the apostle Paul wrote about
his very good friends, Aquila and Priscilla: "Greet
Priscilla and Aquila, my fellow workers in Christ Jesus, who risked their own necks for my life, to whom
not only I give thanks, but also all the churches of the
Gentiles" (Rom. 16:3–4).

Notice that the apostle openly wrote Priscilla's

name before her husband's, not at all afraid that someone would second-guess that relationship as anything but pure.

How different from the stories now surfacing in the newspapers and on television about relationships between men and men, women and women. They create an environment in which it has become extremely difficult for same-sex friendships to be nourished and held up as praiseworthy. Yet just because some homosexual or lesbian relationships of famous people make the headlines, it does not mean that we should not seek same-sex friendships.

Importance of Friendship in Marriage

In fact, Jim Talley in his book on dating relationships, *Too Close, Too Soon,* and on reconciliation after separation or divorce, *Reconcilable Differences,* insists that unless we are able to develop a same-sex friendship as a prelude to marriage, we will be unable to develop the deep friendship needed to sustain a marriage relationship. Once divorce has severed a marriage relationship that did not have a basis in true friendship, the couple needs to go through a period of friendship development with each other before even considering remarriage. In those environments the Master Potter can begin to reshape the relationship into one that will last and be a glory to God.

Recent books for men are now emphasizing that Christian men can and should develop friendly relationships with other men, the kind that has them playing racquetball and golf together. Equally important in today's sex-saturated environment, men, especially leaders, need to develop a circle of friends who will hold them accountable to the Master Potter's design for them.

For Christian women, who tend to seek close relationships through home Bible studies and church activities, it is much easier to develop friends they can confide in and ask to pray for them. If, however, such groups are only opportunities to learn the information in the Bible, they will not provide the relationship shaping the Master Potter is seeking. He had the apostle Paul write: "Bear one another's burdens, and so fulfill the law of Christ" (Gal. 6:2).

Being There for Our Friends

How can we do this? Writing to the Romans, the apostle Paul provided the kind of environment in which this will happen:

> *We then who are strong ought to bear with the*
> *scruples of the weak, and not to please ourselves.*
> *Let each of us please his neighbor for his good,*
> *leading to edification. For even Christ did not*
> *please Himself; but as it is written, "The reproaches*
> *of those who reproached You fell on Me." For*
> *whatever things were written before were written*
> *for our learning, that we through the patience and*
> *comfort of the Scriptures might have hope." (Rom.*
> *15:1–4).*

The Master Potter's "hands" clearly are not only the Holy Spirit He has placed in us, but self-sacrificing friends He has given us to shape us into His image, to be vessels unto honor.

You'll remember that in an earlier chapter I shared

how Leonard and Frances Eilers were the Master Potter's hands in my life. Frances showed up on our doorstep one day after I had submitted to the Master Potter and gave me a specially marked Bible. She knew the temptations of being a Christian in show business, and the Lord used her to reshape my relationship with the Master Potter. I had been headstrong and independent for so long, I needed nurturing in how to discover and then accept the will of the Master Potter.

Frances and Leonard participated in the founding of the Hollywood Christian Group. She was my mentor and support, and Leonard was there for Roy as his "support system" during those traumatic years. I don't think I could have made it without them fulfilling the biblical command to "bear one another's burdens."

Through the years the Master Potter taught me what it means to "pursue the things which make for peace and the things by which one may edify another" (Rom. 14:19); to exercise the love which "bears all things" (1 Cor. 13:7); to "be kind to one another, tenderhearted, forgiving one another, even as God in Christ forgave you" (Eph. 4:32). It took me much longer to come to terms with the apostle Paul's admonition:

Let nothing be done through selfish ambition or conceit, but in lowliness of mind let each esteem others better than himself. Let each of you look out not only for his own interests, but also for the interests of others. (Phil. 2:3–4)

That was not my nature as a person in show business, so the Master Potter had quite a bit of shaping to do before I began to be a vessel unto honor in that way. Even today I agree with the apostle Paul: "Not that I have already attained, or am already perfected; but I press on, that I may lay hold of that for which Christ Jesus has also laid hold of me" (Phil. 3:12).

Those of us who are in the public eye also are aware of another level of relationship, that of leader and follower, of employer and employee, of performer and support staff.

Remember when Roy's contract was up for renewal with Republic Pictures, and he wanted to include the right to participate in television included in the new contract? When the studio head flatly refused to consider it, he was not thinking of what was best for Roy but how to fight that intrusive new form of entertainment, television. As a result, he lost a star actor. Over and over again we have seen men in leadership let personal rivalries and jealousies determine their reactions to their own loss. As the saying goes, they cut off their noses to spite their faces.

Jealousies also develop among those not in leadership. One year when Roy and I were performing in a rodeo I got a taste of this kind of jealousy. Roy was clearly the star of the show, recognized as a top entertainer. Some of the cowboys really resented that, since they went out there on those Brahma bulls at the risk of being gored and losing their lives. I'm sure they thought, "Why should he get all the glory?"

They were really nice to my face, but one night I felt it. Roy, as usual, went out first on Trigger and greeted the crowd. Then he turned to introduce me. My routine was to come barreling out on my horse,

Buttermilk, and greet the crowd. Buttermilk was a fast horse, a little quarterhorse, and I had to be in total command or I might fall off.

That night the drumroll came, and Buttermilk's ears went up. I kicked him to start him into the ring, but just as I did so one of the cowboys stuck his foot out in front of Buttermilk. He shied and jumped sideways, slamming my leg into the side of the chute. I grabbed hold of his mane and with my deep saddle was able to stay seated, but my leg was skinned and bleeding.

I went out and sang the national anthem with Roy and said hello to the people, despite my bleeding leg. Roy had seen the whole thing and was furious, but we were never able to determine who had done it.

The Apostle Paul's Relationships

That's a far cry from the relationship the Master Potter wants us to have with those we work with. I cannot help being amazed by the apostle Paul's relationships with those who were his associates, who traveled the dangerous roads of the Roman Empire with him and were exposed to the persecution preaching the gospel brought.

As you read the following excerpts that illustrate his relationships with his associates, notice the way Paul described those who traveled with him or spent time in Rome with him:

Tychicus, a beloved brother and faithful minister in the Lord. (Eph. 6:21)

*As you also learned from Epaphras, our dear fellow
servant, who is a faithful minister of Christ . . .
(Col. 1:7)*

*Yet I considered it necessary to send to you
Epaphroditus, my brother, fellow worker, and
fellow soldier, but your messenger and the one who
ministered to my need. (Phil. 2:25)*

*But I trust in the Lord Jesus to send Timothy to
you shortly. . . . For I have no one like-minded, who
will sincerely care for your state. (Phil. 2:19, 20)*

Notice how he treated them as his peers, rather
than followers or disciples or underlings. Over and
over he called them his fellow workers. But notice also
how careful he was to give them credit for their contribution, instead of hogging the limelight as the all-
star apostle. That's the humility of Christ, which the
Master Potter wants to instill in each of us through the
work of the Holy Spirit.

Humility the Bottom Line

I'm impressed that the bottom line in all of these
relationships is not only love, but also humility. Without our humility, the Master Potter cannot reshape
our relationships. Without humility, our relationships
cannot develop and become fruitful in serving our
Lord. That's where the Master Potter started in my
life—dealing with my pride and beginning to instill
humility, so I could be Roy's helpmeet and raise the
children in keeping with biblical principles.

All of the reshaping the Master Potter wants to do

in our lives has really only one purpose: that we might be, as the apostle Paul called it, a vessel unto honor, a vessel fit for the Master Potter's use. Unfortunately, I did not recognize that early enough. In fact, when people ask me, "Do you have any real regret in your life? If you could go back, what would you change?" I say, "I would have completely turned to Christ earlier—like after the first real hurt in my life—the desertion by my first husband."

Join me in exploring what it means to be shaped by the Master Potter as we move to the next chapter.

Reflecting on the Shaping

1. What emotional symptoms indicate you need the Master Potter to reshape your relationships?
2. Dale had some very positive family relationships to look back on as models. What kind of relationships served as models for you—and may indicate a major reshaping is needed by the Master Potter?
3. If you are a husband, what can you learn from the experience of Hannah and Elkanah in terms of relationship support in marriage?
4. Why should we make every effort to sustain a marriage relationship shaped by the Master Potter in light of Romans 5:5 and Romans 15:7?

11

A Vessel Fit for
the Master's Use

*I*f you've ever watched a potter work, you'll know there is a stage where the potter stops shaping. His critical eye examines every detail on the object he is making. Finally he picks it up and sets it aside for firing. In the potter's eyes, the object, the vessel, is fit for use by even the most discriminating buyer. That's clearly what the apostle Paul had in mind when he wrote to Timothy: "Therefore if anyone cleanses himself from the latter, he will be a vessel for honor, sanctified and useful for the Master, prepared for every good work" (2 Tim. 2:21).

But what does it really mean to become a vessel fit for the Master Potter's use? The opening statement by the apostle Paul reflects on twenty verses of admonition and challenge regarding what Timothy's life was to be like—and what he was to share with the church he was pastoring. That cleansing, which we'll call shaping, was an ongoing process that reached a stage where the Master Potter could really use the person.

It seems to me that the first prerequisite for becoming a vessel fit for the Master's use is genuine humility. You simply must be humble before your God and know that He is God, that only He can make your life count, really count for His glory. You must be willing to do what the Word of God and His Holy Spirit are telling you to do.

Obedient Acceptance of God's Message

To me, Mary, the mother of Jesus, represents that kind of humility. She was a teenager in the small town of Nazareth, engaged to marry a carpenter. So when an angel appeared to her, it was not exactly an everyday event. Much more surprising even than the angel's appearance was his message: "Rejoice, highly favored one, the Lord is with you; blessed are you among women!" (Luke 1:28)

A cynical young girl might have said to herself, "Wow, what a build-up. Wonder what he wants." Instead, Mary "was troubled at his saying," meaning she couldn't believe what she was hearing. The angel continued:

> *"Do not be afraid, Mary, for you have found favor with God. And behold, you will conceive in your womb and bring forth a Son, and shall call His name JESUS. He will be great, and will be called the Son of the Highest; and the Lord God will give Him the throne of His father David. And He will reign over the house of Jacob forever, and of His kingdom there will be no end." (Luke 1:30–33)*

Hold it, Mary must have been thinking, *a king born to me?* So she responded, "How can this be, since I do not know a man?" (Luke 1:34) Now comes the real puzzler: "The Holy Spirit will come upon you, and the power of the Highest will overshadow you; therefore, also, that Holy One who is to be born will be called the Son of God" (Luke 1:35).

At this stage most girls would either have a big head or be totally stunned by this grand news. But Mary simply answered humbly: "Behold the maidservant of the Lord! Let it be to me according to your word" (Luke 1:38).

That kind of humble acceptance of God's stunning message made her a vessel fit unto the Master's use. Nor is there any indication that Mary made a big thing of the angel's appearance and his message in her social circle. In today's world she probably would have made it onto the "Oprah" show after sharing the news with her friends. Instead she went to see Elizabeth, in keeping with the angel's instruction, and shared with her close relative what God had promised. God honored this humble young woman, a vessel fit for the Master Potter's use, with the great honor of birthing the Messiah and raising Him.

Why Live by the Bible?

Accepting God's Word for us, even when it isn't communicated by an angel, can bring rich rewards for us as well. Unfortunately, according to George Barna's research, only one-third of the age group he calls Baby Boomers are willing to accept that the Bible contains absolute truth—and the generation below that age group is even less willing to accept the Bible as representing absolute truth (*What Americans Believe*, Regal Books, 1991). We have so deified humanity, put our intellect on such a pedestal, that in our pride we

think we can pick and choose from what God has
said, even as Christians. Whatever in the Bible happens to agree with our personal opinion is worth accepting as important for us, but if it clashes with our
own ideas, especially our lifestyle, it obviously cannot
be absolute truth and need not be acted upon.

The person who will say with humility: "Your testimonies also are my delight / And my counselors"
(Ps. 119:24) and "Teach me, O LORD, the way of Your
statutes, / And I shall keep it to the end" (Ps. 119:33),
is the person who will hear God's voice, heed its message, and experience the rewards of obedience.

Yet even when we do accept the Bible as God's
truth for us, we can treat it as though it really is not
that important simply by neglecting it. I have found
myself getting too busy for the Word—and that
means I am too busy for God. I am too busy to just be
in His presence and listen. The psalmist's advice is so
pertinent:

> *Delight yourself also in the LORD,*
> *And He shall give you the desires of*
> *your heart. (Ps. 37:4)*

It's Easy to Neglect the Master

It is so easy to miss Him in the hurly burly of life,
since the Master Potter normally talks to us only in
the still, small voice.

I find that I need to read my Bible regularly. In
addition, I read from various devotional meditations.
Then I talk to the Lord all day as I am doing things.
One of my prized times is when I am driving the car,
for there I can truly be alone with the Lord. But when

I don't do that, I lose the peace that He has given me. All of a sudden I think, "What is going on here? There's something wrong. Have I turned to my own devices again?"

We can make such terrible decisions at such a time. That's why I asked Dr. Norman Vincent Peale one time, "How do you make a hard decision?"

Dr. Peale responded, "Well, I have a cardinal rule. I don't ever make them at night because my defenses are down at night after a tiring day.

"If I am on the road and I have a really crucial decision to make, I get a pencil and paper and make two columns. I write the pros in one column and the cons in the other. Then I take the paper, raise the window if I can, and breathe deeply to get some night air. Then I say, 'Lord, here it is. And I just don't know what to do, what is right. I'm going to depend on you. I am tired tonight, so I am going to depend on you to give me an answer in the morning.' Then I tear up the paper and throw it in the wastebasket. I go to sleep. In the morning, the first solution that comes to me I take as from the Lord. Now sometimes I did not hear right, but God knows my heart was right in what I wanted, and He will overrule."

When we demonstrate humility in submitting to the Master Potter and become pliable under His shaping hands, He starts a whole chain of positive responses in us. These then make us a vessel fit for the Master's use.

The Master Potter Starts in the Home

I'm convinced the Master Potter wants to make us His special vessels in our homes first. Personally, I had been doing my own thing for so long, and been such a failure in many ways, that submission to the Master Potter meant a whole new set of priorities. I determined they were going to be God first, Roy second, the children third, and my work last. That obviously created some conflicts, but as time went on I became more aware of how this priority pattern could work in my life.

It really did start with my commitment to make God supreme in my life. We touched on that in the chapter on priorities, especially in relation to how we included a Christian message in all of our programs. Then there has been my commitment to give Roy his rightful place in our marriage and to work on problems that come up until they are solved.

Our commitment to adopting children, even if they were of different ethnic origin or had physical problems, was a conscious decision to be a vessel fit for the Master's use. You'll remember Sandy, who came from a background of serious abuse and malnourishment. As a result he appeared to be a bit slow. After we took him home we discovered that he had brain damage. It was not serious enough to institutionalize him, but it did mean taking on the role of a humble servant in caring for him.

First we had a terrible time with Sandy's bedwetting. When he went to sleep he was dead to the world and just never woke up in time to go to the bathroom. When he began school, we discovered he had a serious reading problem, so we put him in the Marianne Frostig Remedial School. He came a long way as a result of that help.

Once Sandy learned to read, he became totally focused on military books. Nothing else seemed to interest him. He decided he wanted to become a private first class in the Army, and that's all he lived for. Yet he was so poorly coordinated that he could not learn to ride a bicycle or drive a car. Despite our best efforts he could not shoot straight enough to "hit a barn door." We wondered if he might not simply experience another rejection.

At seventeen, Sandy was failing in high school. He just could not keep up with the rest of the students. But when he asked if we would sign for him to enlist in the Army, since he was under eighteen, we decided to take him in and see if he could make the grade. To our surprise, the Army accepted him.

Sandy made it through boot camp at Fort Polk. He passed the tests, and I was there for his graduation from boot camp when he paraded with his company. They knew he had poor coordination, but in Germany he learned to load and unload a tank. At Fort Polk his sergeant said, "I have been in the military for eighteen years, and I have never seen a boy try as hard as he does."

Prayer Is Most Important

The most important contribution we can make to our children is to pray for them. My maternal grandparents had eight children. Uncle Roy was the oldest, and seven girls were born after him. All the girls made their decision for Christ and joined the church. But Uncle Roy wouldn't. He was a very mischievous boy.

When World War I was declared, Uncle Roy joined the Army and was sent to Germany. All the years since Uncle Roy had been born, my grandmother had been praying for him. She wrote to him constantly, begging him to see a chaplain and confess Christ. She was so afraid he would be killed before he accepted Jesus as his Savior.

Before the war was over and Uncle Roy could come home, my grandmother developed gallstones. They erupted, and peritonitis set in. Her death nearly killed my Uncle Roy. The first thing he did when he came home was to go to church and publicly accept Christ as his Savior, and he stayed true to the Lord for the rest of his life. He is proof that a righteous and faithful mother's prayer "availeth much," even though my grandmother died beseeching the Lord for her son, not knowing what the answer would be.

I am so disheartened at what I hear about goals for women today. I've competed in business and entertainment for many years, and I know that whatever women do, they are never going to be men. I've worked in numerous offices as a secretary. I've been through sexual harassment. Yet for me the real joy came in being the wife of a man who loved me and the mother of children who looked to me for guidance.

I discovered it is almost impossible to have a full-fledged career when there are little children at home, as well as a husband who needs attention. Having a successful career is commendable. Having an attractive home and cooking fine meals are plus points on anyone's chart. But raising a child "in the way he should go" and nurturing a love for God in your child's heart are truly creative accomplishments.

I wrote a book called *Woman* in 1979 and received a lot of flak for it. I went to Atlanta to witness and sing for a group of largely African-American women. While I was there, the phone rang. A reporter from the daily newspaper, *The Atlanta Constitution*, was on the line. She asked me, "What do you think of ERA?" I said, "I don't." She responded, "You are kidding! I've read your books and you've worked since you were seventeen years old."

I said, "Yes, I know. But I just cannot agree with women abdicating the throne of motherhood and their role as wives. We are trying to be men, and we will never be men, no matter how hard we try. God has a place for us, both men and women. I consider it a wonderful privilege to be a woman, with everything that God has endowed me with as a woman."

The reporter wrote a scathing article. As a result there were pickets in front of the auditorium where I sang and witnessed. But I had to say what I considered the truth. And I still do, because I have lived long enough to see the results of women's involvement in the defense industries during World War II. When the men came home from the war, the women were used to getting paychecks for several years. Many of them kept their jobs, undercutting men who needed jobs to care for families. Kids started running on the street, starting a new generation of latchkey kids. I really believe that the results of that trend are on front pages of newspapers and featured in television reports to-day—as gang members and wanton murderers.

True, not every child of every working mother becomes a problem teen. But I believe the trend was set with women working in World War II, creating new levels of income in families, new desires for this world's goods, and more latchkey kids who had no one supervising their after-school activities. Nor were the parents there to make them feel important as family members.

A Reverse Commitment

Parents' commitments to each other and to their children are not the only indication of humble commitment to members of the family. I've also seen a beautiful reverse commitment, that of children to parents. Remember Leonard and Frances Eilers? Like her parents, their daughter Joy also gave her life to ministering Christ to people in the movie industry. A graduate of Princeton, she is a fine pianist. She has traveled widely, giving concerts. Yet even though she is extremely talented, Joy has given years of her life to first both parents, and now to her father, who is ninety-four years old as I write this. Joy says, "As long as my father needs me, I am here for him at the ranch." Indeed a vessel fit unto her Master's use because of her humble service to her father.

But there is also a world beyond the home for many of us. I call it the public world, where we interact with others in our social and church circles, in our places of work. The apostle Paul had something to say in respect to this public world, which he wanted Titus to share with his congregation: "Remind them to be subject to rulers and authorities, to obey, to be ready for every good work, to speak evil of no one, to be peaceable, gentle, showing all humility to all men" (Titus 3:1–2).

He continued that theme in verse 14: "And let our people also learn to maintain good works, to meet urgent needs, that they may not be unfruitful."

The person the Master Potter was shaping into a vessel fit for the Master's use was clearly a caring, gentle person known for his humility. Roy and I often found our gentleness and humility challenged as we moved about. Being considered a "celebrity" means literally becoming public property in the minds of many people—like the woman who stormed into our house right after Robin's funeral to show it to her aunt and introduce her to Roy.

Responsibilities of a Public Person

The responsibilities of being a public figure are literally mind-boggling. That is particularly true if you are a Christian, and you do Christian work, like witnessing for your Lord.

People have asked me, "Don't you get tired of people wanting your autographs?" I reply, "Sometimes. I've been stopped when I am rushing to catch a plane." Numerous times I've said, "Walk along with me while I try to catch the plane."

But for me to be ugly about it and uncaring, indifferent, and callous would be like a cow giving a five-gallon can of milk and then kicking it over.

My goal has been to let the Master Potter use me where He has planted me. I want to "walk worthy of the vocation to which I am called." Some people take that to mean leaving what they are doing to shine for Jesus somewhere else. But I believe God calls some of us to stay there and be salt and light. Even at that, if you really follow the Master Potter, the business you are in may start easing you out, as happened with us on a major network.

If you truly follow the Lord, there are many things you cannot do in show business, particularly in the awful movies being filmed nowadays. The studios simply do not want to make a Christian-oriented film, and Christians do not want to be in films today.

There are times when I got really tired, especially when filming movies. But then I would remember I was in the hands of the Master Potter. I remember one time when we were filming in Big Bear. I was sharing my faith, working with Roy in the picture, and thinking of the children I had left at home. It was like a great big burden on me.

I had a few minutes between scenes involving me, so I took a walk alone one morning. I was desperately tired as I walked down the streets. Suddenly I noticed two little birds accompanying me. They would fly when I walked, and settle down when I rested. I thought, "That's strange."

All of a sudden I stopped and said, "Lord, I'm tired. I am worn out. I am drained. I have nothing more to give. Haven't I done enough? Can I quit?" And as if a light had turned on in my inner being, I heard these words, "Herein is my father glorified in that you bear much fruit." I said, "All right, Father, I'm sorry."

Suddenly I was released and no longer so burdened. I could go back and carry on. The Master Potter's hand had gently lifted me up and strengthened me.

Misunderstanding is another factor in public life that calls for humility and the spirit of a servant. I was invited to be part of the dedication of the reconstructed London Bridge at Lake Havasu in Arizona. I was brought there by a group of eight churches for a Sunday night service. They picked me up in the afternoon and took me to the outdoor site. I sat down at a beat-up piano and played and sang, sharing what Jesus Christ meant to me.

After the program one preacher walked up to me

and said, "Dale, I've never believed you until tonight. Now I believe you." What this minister was telling me was that he had been looking at my life in show business, at the glitz, even though by this time I was really out of it. He had been conditioned to disbelieve the witness of people in that environment, so how could I be believed? By that time the Lord had taught me a lot about humility in the face of misunderstanding, so I simply accepted his statement. But it was part of the Master Potter's shaping me to be a vessel fit for the Master's use.

At such a time it is wise to remember the apostle Paul's admonition to: "pursue righteousness, godliness, faith, love, patience, gentleness" (1 Tim. 6:11).

When we make a definite commitment on our part to do that, then the Master Potter is able to shape us into a vessel fit for His use. Yet I have also discovered that even though you may be a truly useful vessel, the Lord will still put you through the refiner's fire as part of His total process. Sometimes the fire and pressure are really heavy, but think of the molding of the diamond. It is said that the diamond is the toughest gem, so tough that it can cut almost anything—but only because of the pressure it has been under.

Reflecting on the Shaping

1. How do you assess yourself at this point: a vessel unto honor or a vessel unto dishonor? Why?
2. What turns someone into a vessel unto honor?
3. What relationship does being a vessel unto honor have to our study of God's truth in the Bible?
4. What family situations may the Master Potter

want to use to shape you into a genuine vessel unto honor?

5. Where would the Master Potter want you to place your priorities in letting Him shape you into a vessel unto honor?

12

THROUGH THE REFINER'S FIRE

We felt the Refiner's fire again when our Sandy died in Gelhausen, Germany, the night he received his Private First Class stripe. He listened to the temptation offered by his peers to "prove you are a man and deserve that stripe," and in an incident of senseless daring he died. This happened only a year after we lost Debbie in the bus accident.

Does the untimely death of a child like our Robin, or of an early teen like our Debbie, or of a young man like our Sandy, have a divine purpose? Does any seemingly unredeemable situation really carry a purpose because God is preparing us for something greater, or is it just another event on the "being human" calendar?

Great debate material for theologians, of course, but also truly relevant to what each of us experiences. This is particularly true when we believe we have served the Lord rather faithfully. We cannot believe we deserve these extremely difficult and emotionally wrenching experiences. When Roy and I experienced crises in our lives, we faced those questions, at times seriously questioning what God was all about—if He really was involved.

Living a long life does not provide all the answers. Yet reflection does indicate some things the Master Potter clearly achieved in His refining process as He let us bring a Down's syndrome child into the world, let deeply loved Debbie die in a church bus accident, let Sandy die because of an irrational challenge by fellow soldiers, let Roy experience serious health problems, and put me in the hospital with a heart attack.

Gaining Permanent Value

Let's return to our analogy of the potter at work on a clay vessel for a moment. How does a clay vessel get hardened so it can be used in cooking and transporting food? What puts the glaze on that vessel so that it develops a smooth surface with an attractive sheen?

We all know it is in the hot kiln that clay pots are fired for permanence and beauty. That heat produces a chemical reaction that removes moisture and provides a bonding that turns crumbly, easily molded clay into a permanent vessel.

What if that clay pot were to insist that it bypass the intense heat of the kiln? If kept in a dry place, it might retain its shape for a while, but it would soon crumble. Yet properly fired clay produces vessels that can be dug up thousands of years later with inscriptions still clearly legible on them. The heat of the kiln gave them permanence.

Similarly, the refiner's fire is the Master Potter's process for purifying the Christian for more effective service at home, in the church and community, and beyond. I have never found the purifying process pleasant, but I have learned that the Master Potter knows what He is about.

Although it is not always the case, I find that, as with clay vessels, we experience the purifying, hardening fire after the Master Potter has done His major reshaping in our lives. At the time, we consider those shaping experiences the refining fire, and in some ways they are, but we are not ready for the true refining fire until He has effected His major shaping in us.

The Purpose of Trials

What is the refining process all about? Here's how James puts it in his letter:

> *My brethren, count it all joy when you fall into various trials, knowing that the testing of your faith produces patience. But let patience have its perfect work, that you may be perfect and complete, lacking nothing. (James 1:2–4).*

When Art Rush came onto the set at Seattle to inform us that the network wanted us to cut out the name of Christ in our God and country song, "How Great Thou Art," we knew this was a trial. Much more was at stake than just pulling out one name in a song. This was an attempt to quickly destroy our attempt at a Christian witness, despite the network's promise that we could do whatever we wanted on the show. But we also knew that if we insisted on keeping our witness songs on the program, there was very little likelihood of our contracts being renewed. The temptation was to give in so we could stay on the air and put bread on the table.

Saying no quickly to the network's request, and then seeing God provide for us in other ways, strengthened us. It hardened our resolve to always have a witness in our shows, no matter where we were. And it prepared us for the request of the manager of Madison Square Garden that we remove the cross from the set while we sang "Peace in the Valley." Roy and I did not have to think twice about it.

Too Great a Price?

We paid the price for our witness to Christ. Yet we did not consider that too great a price, for we considered the price Jesus Christ paid for our salvation much greater. I knew how I had felt before I gave my life to Christ, and how restless I had been inside. It seemed as if I was always not doing what I should do, and doing what I shouldn't do. But when the Master Potter gave me peace and began shaping me, that restlessness disappeared and I experienced true inner peace.

You may be thinking that you cannot really relate to that, since your life is not in the public eye as ours was. The fact is that all of us face trials if we are living for the Lord. We go through experiences that don't make any sense to us until years after we have been through them. My son, Tom, went through one of those truly mortifying and humiliating experiences that, on the surface, should never have happened.

Tom taught music in the public school system for twenty-six years when a teacher's strike over issues he did not agree with prompted him to leave teaching.

He became the Minister of Music at Arcade Baptist Church in Sacramento. After providing twelve years of outstanding leadership in music there, he determined that he had about three good years left of full-time service. He and Barbara agreed he should spend it back in the classroom that had given him so many good years. It would also increase his pension benefits as a bonus.

Our foster daughter, Marion, worked as executive-secretary to the superintendent of the Palmdale school district, and she helped find him a position in the district. After a tearful farewell, with many requests to change their minds, Tom and Barbara moved all of their household goods 450 miles south to Palmdale.

Nothing, however, went right for Tom and Barbara in housing and other aspects of living and working in the Palmdale area. Tom says, "We soon developed roadblocks of doubt that we had moved out of the will of God. For two weeks we had a heart-rending experience of praying that God would make His will clear to us. We concluded we had acted on our personal wills, not in keeping with the will of God. The people of Arcade Baptist made it clear that we would be welcome to return to our previous church positions, I as Minister of Music and Barbara as senior organist."

The members of Arcade came down and moved all of their furniture back and restored them to their former positions. Yet it was a most embarrassing, even humiliating, experience for someone who had served the Lord so many years. Tom also felt great remorse for having let Marion down. And both felt they had let a lot of friends down at Arcade because they had not really understood the will of God.

Trials Develop Understanding

The Master Potter was clearly using that as part of the refining process, however, for when they retired after three years the opportunity at Black Forest Academy in Germany opened up. Then he could use his gifts to teach music in an international Christian school, serving the educational needs of missionaries' kids from thirty-one countries in Europe, Africa, and the Middle East. These kids had also experienced a lot of disappointments. Tom and Barbara could serve them out of genuine humility, recognizing their own fallibility as Christians.

Such humiliation is clearly part of the Master Potter's shaping process to create dependence upon Him. In an earlier chapter we touched on the failure of the apostle Peter, the marring of his testimony, when he denied his Lord three times in the courtyard of the high priest. Let's go back in time to the day the Master Potter saw two boats standing on the shore of the Lake of Gennesaret, with the fishermen busy mending their nets nearby.

Jesus had already developed a significant following, for a "multitude" of people was pressing in on Him to hear Him speak. No doubt Peter, James, and John had already heard of Jesus. In fact, they may already have personally heard and believed His words. But they had to keep bread on the table for their families, so they had gone fishing. Unfortunately, the previous night they had caught nothing, a most unusual experience for these veteran fishermen.

Peter in the Spotlight

When Jesus approached, not even Peter knew what the Master had in mind. But he was glad to offer his boat when Jesus asked if He could use it as a pulpit. Peter gladly moved it offshore and away from the crowds. With the water acting like a megaphone, Jesus could easily speak to a large crowd.

This was tremendous exposure. After all, how often can you get a "multitude" focusing on your fishing enterprise? Clearly, this was great advertising.

Then Jesus turned Peter's world upside down. After addressing the multitude, Jesus asked Peter to "launch out into the deep" (Luke 5:4) and let down the net to catch some fish. It was all fine and good for Jesus to ask for his boat as a pulpit, but to request they resume fishing in broad daylight, in front of the crowd, clearly overstepped the bounds of propriety. After all, Peter was the fisherman, and he and his associates had fruitlessly fished all night—and everyone knew fish were difficult to catch when the sun came out.

Peter's loss of control over the situation could prove most embarrassing if they put out the nets and caught nothing. The Master wouldn't catch the flak; the crowd had probably not heard Him give the command to Peter, and would blame Peter. The last thing Peter needed was a display of ineptitude.

Yet Peter had also developed a genuine faith in this remarkable teacher. So he said: "Master, we have toiled all night and caught nothing; nevertheless at Your word I will let down the net" (Luke 5:5).

Overwhelming Bounty

Peter moved from independence to dependence, the "at Your word, Lord" stage that all of us must reach before the Master Potter finds us a vessel unto honor. Peter pushed off into the deeper water and let down the net, while the crowd wondered what in the world was going on. I suspect Peter was also skeptical that anything would develop. When they started pulling up the nets, however, they were bulging with fish. In fact, the nets were overwhelmed and started tearing. So Peter and his associates signaled for help, and the men in the other boat came out to help them bring a huge catch on board.

Under normal circumstances, I suspect, Peter may have done some strutting. After all, the whole crowd had watched this unbelievable scene as nets full of flopping and struggling fish were hauled in over the edge of the boats. Today's TV news cameras would have had a field day. Yet the Master Potter had gotten through to Peter at a very deep level. He had put the fire to this self-sufficient, cocky fisherman and out came, at least for the moment, a humble, contrite person who fell down on his knees at Jesus' feet and said: "Depart from me, for I am a sinful man, O Lord!" (Luke 5:8).

Jesus knew that Peter had gone through the first stage of refinement, necessary to make him a disciple. Other experiences would continue the refinement, with the denial the final "firing" of the human clay that was Peter so he could move from disciple to apostle.

The Scriptures record only one more incident that casts Peter in a negative light. He chooses to side with his Jewish friends against the Gentiles at Antioch, and the apostle Paul had to confront him publicly about his anti-Gentile attitude. Apparently Peter took it to heart, for Paul doesn't mention it further.

An Honor Withdrawn

I got into one of those situations where the Master Potter put the fire to my pride. The year I was chosen "Mother of the Year" in California, I went to New York for the annual convention of the sponsoring organization. There I was nominated for "National Mother of the Year," a tremendous honor. No doubt our multinational family contributed to my receiving the awards. The night before the final award ceremony I was asked to give my testimony. Unaware of the furor it would cause, I told about my divorces.

The sponsors quickly informed me that they would have to withdraw my name from nomination for "National Mother of the Year." They had an absolute rule that no divorced woman, no matter how great she subsequently became as a mother, could be National Mother of the Year.

For me, this was a tremendous emotional setback—and a most humbling experience. Yet I was so grateful they had acted immediately when they discovered my divorces, because they were right. Our country is so desperately in need of stable homes. I won't even accept a position as deaconess in the church because of my divorces. That doesn't stop my witness, but I believe I'm disqualified from a form of service in which the participants are to be role models in the local church.

Establishing Purpose and Focus

Going through the Master Potter's refining fire has a way of helping us establish purpose and focus for our life. When Robin died and my book *Angel Unaware* was published, the Lord gave me an extraordinary opportunity to witness His sustaining grace during times of great trial. Without that, I would have been just another entertainer alongside my husband. But I was able to get Down's syndrome children out of the closet, to get their parents the help they needed. As time went on, I discovered this spilled over to all disabled children of whom the public was ashamed.

When Debbie was killed in a bus accident, we went through shock and intense grief. Earlier I shared how I doubted God's goodness for a brief period— and how Roy struggled with what he considered a senseless death. But again the Lord opened a door for a new level of witness, this time to parents who had lost a child in a similar way.

Sandy's death in Germany could have totally devastated us, since it again was a needless death. The Master Potter had prepared us for this refinement by having Sandy write us a letter, which we received a week before his death. In it he expressed his commitment to the Savior and to establishing a Christian home with the young woman to whom he was engaged. This became another kind of witness to our total dependence on God for life and breath—and His sustaining presence in the midst of trial. Books on

Debbie and Sandy helped to spread the message to people I could not reach through personal appearances.

You get right down to the nitty gritty when you are humiliated, as I was in the "National Mother of the Year" incident. You get down to what counts, where you can express something because you have been through it. You've been on the Master Potter's wheel and in the refining fire.

The difference in the "before" and "after" parts of the refiner's fire is seen in an experience I had with Art Linkletter. After I wrote *Angel Unaware*, Art had me as a guest on his program. The purpose was to talk about the book, for it was making quite a splash. On the program, Art asked me, "Tell me what made you write this book" (a rather standard question for interviewers of authors). I took the opportunity to tell him and the audience about giving my life to Christ, how His presence in my life had sustained me during the trauma of losing Robin after having her with us for two years. Then I shared how God had held me up after her death. Art was taken aback, for he had not expected this clear a witness.

Since experiencing trials through his own children, Art has supported Christian efforts to deal with drugs and other family problems. However, he no longer has his own program; it's funny how show business will finally ease you out once you fall in love with Jesus Christ.

It seems I had suffered enough after the death of three children to reach a stage where the Lord simply wanted to use me for some years. No significant trauma struck our family while I criss-crossed the country sharing what the Master Potter is all about in our lives. I got the feeling that maybe we were home free, when Roy ended up in the hospital again.

In 1978, Roy had triple by-pass heart surgery, just ahead of what could have been a severe heart attack. The Lord used this to teach me another level of patience, to "let go and let God handle it," especially since I was scheduled to host a tour of five pastors and a huge crowd of Christians to Israel not long after his surgery. But the Lord had Roy home before I had to leave.

In 1990, Roy suffered another setback; this time he had to have surgery on a large aneurysm on his aorta. This was a most difficult experience, especially since the surgeon informed me the night before surgery that Roy might not make it through the surgery. Our pastor, Bill Hansen, prayed with Roy and me before the operation. At that point Roy calmly said, "Whatever the Lord wills, I am ready. I am not afraid."

While recovering, Roy developed the flu, which progressed into pneumonia. That was a hard trial indeed, but the Master Potter delivered him from that as well.

The Master Potter refocused my attention when in May 1992, He let me experience a violent heart attack. I was in excruciating pain in the hospital. Having a baby was child's play compared to the pain I was experiencing. I said to the Lord, "Are You there? Lord, are You there? Get me out of here. If You are going to take me, take me now. I cannot make it anymore."

Suddenly I said to the Master Potter, "Was this the way it was with You on the cross? Did You suffer like this?" Then I said, "You did not do anything to deserve Your pain. Forgive me for saying, 'Get me out of here.'"

By that time the nurses had inserted needles in me all over, and I lost consciousness for a time. The next day my lungs filled up, and I could not breathe. They ran tests and discovered that a valve had been damaged badly and was letting blood get back into my lungs. Only when they went in again and put a steel ring into place to stop the valve from malfunctioning did my lungs begin to clear.

Through all of these refining experiences I have learned to withdraw into myself, into the small, quiet center of my being, in complete trust in God. There I simply "wait upon the Lord," trusting Him to work out events in His faultless timing. Neither Roy nor I can say we are really healthy anymore, but we are determined to serve our Lord as long as He permits.

Each of us has personal refining fire experiences. The Master Potter knows exactly how high to turn up the fire. That's why the apostle Paul could write:

No temptation has overtaken you except such as is common to man; but God is faithful, who will not allow you to be tempted beyond what you are able, but with the temptation will also make the way of escape, that you may be able to bear it. (1 Cor. 10:13)

What is the purpose of the refining fire? There are many, but the ultimate purpose on earth seems to be to make us fit to be on display to the world. Scary thought? Let's examine that idea in the next chapter.

Reflecting on the Shaping

1. What adds permanence and luster to a piece of clay pottery?
2. Which experience would you identify as being used by the Master Potter to refine you?
3. What is the purpose of the refining fire according to James 1:2–4?
4. What might have been the purpose for the humiliation Tom and Barbara experienced when they moved to Palmdale?
5. What can we learn from Peter's experience with Jesus to help us in frustrating, humiliating situations?

13

ON DISPLAY FOR THE MASTER

*H*ave you ever wandered through one of those large pottery display rooms in a major tourist area? Whether it's in Williamsburg, Virginia, or Old Town in San Diego, California, you'll quickly notice that a majority of the clay containers or vases are utilitarian reddish-brown in color. Their purpose is rather basic, to provide a container for soil and plants or a flower arrangement.

Yet when you go into the airport gift shop in Phoenix, Arizona, for example, you will see some beautifully painted clay vessels on display. They are clearly objects of art, designed to help beautify a room. Travelers take them home to their wives or give them to their friends as special gifts.

Most of us Christians consider ourselves rather plain and ordinary. We are happy to stay out of the spotlight so we don't need to feel self-conscious about our too-long noses, mousy hair, or pear-shaped bodies. We'll gladly let the "beautiful people" take the spotlight, even while we envy their physical beauty.

Every Vessel on Display

Yet even the clay pot into which you put the ficus tree you set in the corner of your living room is on display. Most of us are rather picky even about that kind of pot, for its shape and perfection of detail speak volumes about our own good taste, or lack thereof. There is a certain beauty in simplicity that speaks of the potter's careful workmanship.

The apostle Paul speaks to this when he wrote about Christians: "But we have this treasure in earthen vessels, that the excellence of the power may be of God and not of us" (2 Cor. 4:7).

What Paul was clearly implying is that when the Master Potter shapes us for His service, He is concerned that we do not become proud of our own beauty, of our intellectual gifts, of our education and achievements. When we are on display in the world, those watching us need to become more excited about the power of God working through us than about who we are.

For me, someone who was already in show business when I committed myself to the Master Potter, this was not an easy lesson to learn. I was so used to showing my profile to the camera at a very specific angle, of having my face and hair prepared as though they were all-important, of giving my acting the most intense scrutiny. After a day of shooting was done, I'd spend time looking at the "rushes," examining every move I had made, every facial angle, to improve my professional performance.

An experience I had during the second World War illustrates how unimportant our exterior display is when the heart is right. I was sitting in the bulkhead seat of an airplane going from Chicago to California. In the seat next to me was Eleanor Roosevelt. In my weakness, and because of Hollywood's influence, when I looked at her I thought, *She is so homely.* But then I started talking with her, and she started asking me questions. Out of her eyes came such caring concern that I was overwhelmed. She had a sweetness and a caring that just spilled out—and she was not unattractive anymore.

I was reading a prayer book at the time, so I asked her to sign the flyleaf, one of only two people I have ever asked for an autograph.

The Master Potter used others as well to reshape my attitude. You'll remember how surprised I was when Dick Halverson refused to take any credit for his singing, simply saying, "Praise the Lord." After all, he had sung extremely well, communicating most effectively the message of Christ. Why would he not accept my words of appreciation? From his example, from how others served in humility as servants, and from my study of the Bible, I came to realize that humble service to the Master Potter deflects attention from us to the Lord.

Faith on Display

I discovered that one key to being a vessel unto honor through a humble, servant attitude is to be aware that we are on display at all times for the Master Potter. No matter how insignificant we are, someone is watching us and evaluating our Master Potter's ability by how effectively we have let Him shape us.

For instance, I used to smoke, not much until I got into the pictures. But sitting around and waiting for the crew to change the lights meant interminable waits, and smoking was simply something to do. I never enjoyed it a whole lot, taking one to three puffs and then putting the cigarette out.

Shortly after I was married to Roy I took out a cigarette to have a smoke. One of the children said, "I wish you wouldn't smoke. My mommy didn't smoke."

Suddenly I realized I was on display, and it was not a pleasing sight to the children. My smoking was an added negative if I wanted to win them over and be their mother. So I said to her, "I will not smoke another cigarette."

You'll remember my telling about Marguerite Hamilton and her daughter, Nancy, the little girl with the enlarged feet and hands. To the casual observer, what was on display was a misshapen little girl. Yet those of us who got to know Nancy and her mother recognized that her great courage and faith in God's provision was really what was on display. They became the Master Potter's object lesson of caring commitment to one's child no matter what the child looked like. That's the display I needed to see to have my attitudes changed by the Master Potter before Robin arrived as a Down's syndrome child.

After Robin's birth I was having one of my down days. Where did I go? Visit one of the movie stars, one of the great preachers of the day? No, I got into the car and drove to Santa Monica, where Marguerite was managing a small motel. I brought them some meat, vegetables, and fruit from our ranch, since we had our own orchard, beef cattle, and vegetable garden.

Yet I always left with more than I brought, for I always left with my faith renewed, my courage strengthened. Nancy's implicit faith that God would supply their every need challenged me, who had a lot more available, to trust God for every need in my life.

Some time ago I was challenged by another example of parents "on display" by the way they cared for their Down's syndrome son. I invited Chris Burke, the star of "Life Goes On," for an interview on my television program, "A Date with Dale." I was impressed with Chris, for the television show is almost built around him. Later I had the privilege of presenting him with one of the two annual awards the Motion Picture Association gives to actors or actresses who have contributed something special to the motion picture industry.

At the awards ceremony I got up and said, "You cannot possibly know how warm my heart is to be a part of this presentation to Chris Burke, a Down's syndrome person." I was thinking of how they had told me that Robin would never progress beyond the age of five in her mental capacity—and here I was giving an award to a young man with Down's syndrome for his contribution to the movie industry. Just as soon as I used the term Down's syndrome, Chris yelled from the head table, "I'm not a Down's. I'm an up!"

Chris's father and mother, who are Catholics, just poured themselves into this boy. The results were on display, honoring their Christian commitment to their son.

Roy and I are so thrilled at how the Master Potter has been at work in the lives of our children. Yes, we lost three, but the others have all come to know the Lord and have a lively faith in Him. I've already shared that Tom and Barbara went to Germany for one year to serve at a Christian academy for children of missionaries. All his life he has given Christ first place, and now that is being reflected in his children as well.

Cheryl, Roy's oldest daughter, is married and lives about an hour from us. There's such a warmth in her home when I walk in. Although initially as a child she was standoffish with me, I now have a real closeness with Cheryl. I get wonderful birthday, Christmas, and Easter cards from her, all with verses that express gratitude, which really gets to me.

Linda Lou, Roy's second daughter, has always had a feeling for the underdog, the less fortunate. She was the one who noticed Nancy's crippled feet first, and called me to invite Marguerite and Nancy into our house. Today Linda Lou is a pastor's wife, ministering to older people in a church near Fresno.

Dusty (Roy Jr.) married a fine Christian woman and was in general construction. When our agent, Art Rush, died, Roy asked if Dusty would move here and help as manager of the museum and set up our appointments. Dusty has been a singer and had his own band at one time, so he knows what is involved. He is doing an outstanding job, while staying active in sports activities with children. He is on the board of the Happy Trails Foundation for Abused Children as well.

Dodie, our little Choctaw adoptee, is married to the son of a Church of Christ pastor, who also has some Indian blood in his family. They, too, live about an hour away, where Dodie is very active in her church. They sponsor a Bible class in their home as well.

We were told at the home where we adopted her that Dodie was three-quarters Choctaw and one-

quarter Scottish/Irish. However, I found her birth
mother when she was fourteen or fifteen, and through
that her grandmother, who is active in Indian affairs
in Los Angeles. She told Dodie, "You are full-blooded
Choctaw."

For a white couple to adopt an Indian child is today a contentious issue among Indians. One day
when I had Dodie on location with me, a Cherokee
said to me, "You know, you have robbed her of her
heritage." Much later I told Dodie about this experience, and she sent me the most beautiful letter. She
wrote, "I didn't give up anything being your daughter, despite my Indian heritage. If I had to do it again,
I would choose you."

I mentioned earlier that our foster daughter,
Marion, is employed as executive-secretary in the
Palmdale School District. She is also married and a
wonderful Christian, active in her church.

Our children are now our greatest joy, along with
our sixteen grandchildren and twenty-seven great-
grandchildren, with two more on the way!

A Different Kind of Display

There is another level at which we are on display
for the Master Potter, and that is through the people
we minister to. The apostle Paul wrote to the Corinthians in that connection: "You are our epistle written
in our hearts, known and read by all men; clearly you
are an epistle of Christ, ministered by us, written not
with ink but by the Spirit of the living God" (2 Cor.
3:2–3).

In his first letter to the Corinthians, he expressed

himself similarly: "For you are the seal of my apos-tleship in the Lord" (1 Cor. 9:2).

From the apostle Paul's perspective, the people who had come to know Christ through his ministry were on display as validation of God's calling on his life. I wouldn't dare compare myself with the great apostle, but I, too, see people whose lives were changed as a result of my books and public witness, validating God's call. When I think of the thousands of letters from grateful parents who saw their Down's syndrome child in another light, who were given the courage to go on, I'm truly grateful. When I think of the disabled children, now adults, who were helped to a new life through my efforts on their behalf, I'm thankful for my "display."

The Master Potter took a badly marred vessel and reshaped it for a truly worldwide ministry that far surpassed anything I could have done on my own. To Him be the glory!

On Display in the Home

I believe that one area in which Christians are on display is in the area of marriage. True, Christians are a little less likely to become divorced, but the percent-age is still shockingly high. In an earlier chapter I wrote about my changed attitude about divorce after I submitted my life to the Master Potter. I was abso-lutely committed to making my marriage to Roy work.

In the forty-five years since I committed myself to Roy for the rest of my life, attitudes toward divorce in America have changed dramatically. Today more than half of all new marriages will end in divorce. So many people seek divorces because of what they describe as *incompatibility*. I call it *failure to learn effective communication*.

That's where I believe those of us who have achieved happy, long-term marriages can be the Master Potter's display of what it takes to stay married. In his book *The Marriage Savers*, Mike McManus presents ways in which we can all help save marriages. One way is to mentor couples whose marriages are troubled. This mentoring is most effective if a pastor provides the leadership to bring together couples who have made it with couples whose marriages are in trouble. Our granddaughter, Candi Halberg, and her husband Todd front "Marriage Ministries" in Littleton, Colorado, near Denver.

Mike McManus tells of a Florida church where the pastor took such an initiative and brought together seven couples as lay mentors. Of the thirty-three deeply troubled marriages they got involved in, none broke up over the next several years.

On Display Through Choices We Make

We are also on display for the Master in the choices we make as those who are being shaped for His service. These choices are illustrated repeatedly in the apostle Paul's letters. Ephesians 4 provides a lengthy list of choices that put us on display, reminding the Ephesians, and us, that they will not be able to make good choices without putting on a new man:

> *Put off, concerning your former conduct, the old man which grows corrupt according to the deceitful lusts, and be renewed in the spirit of your mind,*

and that you put on the new man which was
created according to God, in true righteousness and
holiness. (Eph. 4:22–24)

In the power of this new person, "created according to God," they were to put away lying, anger,
thievery, corrupt words, bitterness, clamor, and evil
speaking. Quite a list of behaviors that would bring
disgrace on the name of the Lord, who made us! But
what God wants us to display is kindness, tender-
heartedness, forgiveness—beautiful qualities that
bring honor to our Lord.

One of the entertainers who knows firsthand what
the apostle Paul is talking about is Gavin MacLeod of
"Love Boat" fame. After both Gavin and his wife,
Patti, came to the Lord some years ago, they had to
turn down a lot of "opportunities" that would drag
them back to their old way of life.

Gavin told me, "Just last week we turned down an
enormous opportunity. We had been praying to the
Lord that morning and asking Him if He would
please send some money our way because we really
happened to need it at the moment. Later that day my
agent called from New York with an offer of a prestigious part in a musical in Atlantic City. The problem
was that it featured and glorified sin. I called our pastor, Jack Hayford, to talk it over because I felt we just
couldn't do it. He gave us great advice, 'You're being
tempted because you need the money, just as Jesus
was tempted in the wilderness.'

"So we turned it down, and wouldn't you know
that just a little while later somebody visited from
New York, where they're doing some new theater,

and he offered me the same part in the very same musical! The devil just doesn't give up."

Satan certainly would love to destroy the testimony we have when we are on display for the Master Potter.

Death to Ego

Yes, being on display for the Master all the time is not easy. But I keep on asking the Lord humbly to get me out of the way so He can be seen in me. When I gave my life to Christ, I died. My ego died. Every now and then it raises its ugly head, but I deal with it by saying, "Down, boy." I tell myself, "This is the Lord's work, so He must get the glory."

The apostle Paul presented our passage through the world as Christians in a truly beautiful way in his letter to the Corinthians:

> *Now thanks be to God who always leads us in triumph in Christ, and through us diffuses the fragrance of His knowledge in every place. For we are to God the fragrance of Christ among those who are being saved and among those who are perishing. To the one we are the aroma of death leading to death, and to the other the aroma of life leading to life. (2 Cor. 2:14–16)*

What a beautiful image in a fragrance-oriented society. Amazing how up-to-date some of the apostle's word pictures are. The truth in the image is that some people respond to our witness negatively, only to experience eternal death. Others respond positively, and they gain life eternal.

Going through the refining fire, being on display to the world, are both part of God's great purpose for us, to be with Him in glory. That's when all the imperfections will be removed and we will truly be vessels unto honor for the Master Potter.

Reflecting on the Shaping

1. Where do you feel you are especially on display for the Master in today's world?

2. What can we learn from 2 Corinthians 4:7 about our role as vessels in God's plan?

3. Identify someone with the kind of sweet, caring inner spirit that Dale found in Eleanor Roosevelt. What can you learn from this person in respect to being on display?

4. How does it make you feel when you think about being on display for the Master?

5. After reading 2 Corinthians 3:2, ask yourself whose "epistle" you are as a Christian.

14

PERFECTED AT LAST

One day I was sitting quietly doing some reading when Roy said, "I want to ask you something."

I responded, "Shoot."

He asked, "What are we going to do in heaven?"

"God knows exactly what we are going to do in heaven," I said. "For one thing, we are going to praise Him all the time. We'll tell Him how much we love Him and how delighted we are to be there."

Roy persisted, "But what are we going to do? In the first place, I want to be married to you in heaven."

I said, "But you don't understand. There is no marriage or giving in marriage in heaven. We are as the angels in heaven."

Roy remembered our dog, an old Weimaraner who had been involved in an accident and could not do much. He just sat around and grinned all the time, scratching himself.

"You mean I am going to have to sit and grin and scratch for an eternity?" Roy asked, putting on the worst possible face to our activity in heaven.

Looking for a City

We all have questions about heaven, and the more active we are, the more we wonder if it will be genuinely exciting for an eternity. Yet even the heroes of the faith in the Old Testament were looking forward to the glories and rewards of heaven. We read about Abraham.

By faith he [Abraham] dwelt in the land of promise as in a foreign country, dwelling in tents with Isaac and Jacob, the heirs with him of the same promise; for he waited for the city which has foundations, whose builder and maker is God. (Heb. 11:9–10)

Abraham remained a nomad all his life, never moving into a permanent dwelling. God had called him to leave home for a piece of the world that was totally foreign to him, and that sense of being a foreigner all his life kept his eye on what God had for him beyond death. He looked forward to permanence, to a city made by God for those faithful ones who accepted what God has for them on earth.

The apostle Paul was another traveler whose most permanent dwelling place seemed to be as a prisoner in Rome. Yes, he stayed in Ephesus for two years, but that was clearly planned as a church-planting interlude. So he moved on when the church had developed enough maturity to succeed without him.

On top of that, Paul experienced horrendously difficult circumstances. I mean, who would want to stick around on earth with the following list of adventures?

Are they ministers of Christ?—I speak as a fool—I

am more: *in labors more abundant, in stripes above
measure, in prisons more frequently, in deaths
often. From the Jews five times I received forty
stripes minus one. Three times I was beaten with
rods; once I was stoned; three times I was
shipwrecked; a night and a day I have been in the
deep; in journeys often, in perils of waters, in perils
of robbers, in perils of my own countrymen, in
perils of the Gentiles, in perils in the city, in perils
in the wilderness, in perils in the sea, in perils
among false brethren; in weariness and toil, in
sleeplessness often, in hunger and thirst, in fastings
often, in cold and nakedness. (2 Cor. 11:23–27)*

Anybody ready to match that litany of horrors? It's
clear the book of Acts gives only an occasional snap-
shot of this intrepid missionary. So what is he looking
forward to?

*For here we have no continuing city, but we seek
the one to come. (Heb. 13:14)*

Nothing Passive About Waiting

That seeking for the heavenly city is no passive
waiting for God to drop it out of heaven, or boost us
up into it whenever we please. The apostle Paul (I'm
assuming he wrote the book of Hebrews) indicated
that the knowledge that we are bound for a celestial
city should be a motivating factor to personal purity,
to a life committed to humbly serving the Master Potter, to worship:

Therefore by Him let us continually offer the

sacrifice of praise to God, that is, the fruit of our
lips, giving thanks to His name. But do not forget
to do good and to share, for with such sacrifices God
is well pleased. (Heb. 13:15–16)

That little word *therefore* follows immediately after
his indication that we are seeking the city to come,
indicating that in the light of our destination, we
ought to begin to praise and worship now. After all,
that is what we will be primarily doing, if John's
Revelation of Jesus Christ can be believed. And I
know we'll all rejoice at not having to fend off the
temptations Satan lays on us, or deal with the natural
desires of our flesh as fallen human beings.

Glad to Join the Choir

I'm looking forward to just joining the celestial
choir and singing to my heart's content. No longer
will I be considered a "star," with the spotlight shining on me, for Jesus is the only star there (as He ought
to be here!). Even though it seems a good part of the
worship of God and the Lamb, Jesus Christ, in heaven
is done by angelic beings and elders, there are clearly
choirs of the redeemed involved.

At one point there are 144,000 who have the Father's name written on their foreheads (Rev. 14:1) who
join an orchestra of harps (v. 2) in a joyous expression
of praise:

They sang as it were a new song before the throne,
before the four living creatures, and the elders; and
no one could learn that song except the hundred

and forty-four thousand who were redeemed from
the earth. (Rev. 14:3)

In the following chapter of Revelation, we again
have a large group who are not clearly identified, but
who:

sing the song of Moses, the servant of God, and the
song of the Lamb, saying:

"Great and marvelous are Your works,
Lord God Almighty!
Just and true are Your ways,
O King of the saints!
Who shall not fear You, O Lord,
    and glorify Your name?
For You alone are holy.
For all nations shall come and worship before
    You,
For Your judgments have been manifested.
(Rev. 15:3–4)

Both Roy and I are now of an age where we are
truly looking forward to joining that choir. Roy may
add a yodel now and then in his cowboy style, I will
sing in more traditional fashion, and our grandchildren will want to be in a contemporary style choir, but
the form will not be the issue.

Perfected at Last

We will finally be perfected by the Master Potter,
on display for God Himself and all His saints. That is
clearly one reason why the Master Potter is so active

in shaping us throughout life: "that He might present her [the church] to Himself a glorious church, not having spot or wrinkle or any such thing, but that she should be holy and without blemish" (Eph. 5:27).

I'm looking forward to seeing Roy there, with his new heart and new body, rejoicing in meeting Robin, Debbie, and Sandy again, as well as other members of our large family. But I'm also looking forward to seeing other faithful servants of God there.

I think of Ralph Hoopes and his wife, Georgia Lee, a very pretty girl with a good voice. They both were under contract to Warner Brothers when they met Jesus and accepted Him as Lord. She gave up acting so she could just be a witness for Christ. She was used in a number of Billy Graham films as a result. He worked in the crusades as a witness for Christ, finally founding a church.

I'm looking forward as well to meeting another show business personality who gave up her career in the movies when she accepted the Savior: Colleen Townsend. She was a promising star when she started coming to the Hollywood Christian Group. There she met Louis Evans, Jr., fell in love with him, and married him. She gave up her movie career to become a minister's wife and a mother. She became a witness through her books as well.

I'm also looking forward to worshiping God with Frances and Leonard Eilers and Joy, just like we used to worship together here.

Still Enjoying His Goodness

That doesn't mean I'm not enjoying my life now. In fact, even at eighty-one years of age I'm enjoying life very, very much because I have such a backlog of experiences to enjoy. The Master Potter has conditioned me to rejoice in what He has done, rather than complain about my aches and pains. True, the pain connected with my heart attack was not pleasurable at all, but He restored me to an amazingly active life after that, so that all I can do is praise Him.

Do I fear death? No. In fact, at times when I've been so desperately tired I did not know if I could go on, I have prayed, "How long, O Lord?" I've been on programs with people who have had deathbed experiences and have come back, reporting wonderful sights. But I do not fear death because I am sure of my salvation through the Master Potter. I just thank the Master Potter for being so gracious to me all these years—and promising me a home in heaven, in the city built by God.

Because of that, I also don't worry about the state of our economy, about our people. The Bible says that God "lifts nations up and puts nations down." I'll let Him take care of the world while I rejoice in my corner of it—and the promise of being perfected at last when I meet my Savior face to face.

The apostle John gave us such a beautiful promise in connection with that: "Beloved, now we are children of God; and it has not yet been revealed what we shall be, but we know that when He is revealed, we shall be like Him, for we shall see Him as He is" (1 John 3:2).

I can live in anticipation of that gladly!

Reflecting on the Shaping

1. What are your expectations for when you get to heaven?

2. According to Hebrews 11:9–10, why was Abraham willing to stay in tents as a nomad throughout his life?

3. What things can we do as we seek the city to come according to Hebrews 13:15–16?

4. Which of your talents/abilities might the Master Potter use in heaven?

5. What does God want to achieve in us before we are ready for heaven, according to Ephesians 5:27?